SpringerBriefs in Computer Science

SpringerBriefs present concise summaries of cutting-edge research and practical applications across a wide spectrum of fields. Featuring compact volumes of 50 to 125 pages, the series covers a range of content from professional to academic.

Typical topics might include:

- A timely report of state-of-the art analytical techniques
- A bridge between new research results, as published in journal articles, and a contextual literature review
- A snapshot of a hot or emerging topic
- An in-depth case study or clinical example
- A presentation of core concepts that students must understand in order to make independent contributions

Briefs allow authors to present their ideas and readers to absorb them with minimal time investment. Briefs will be published as part of Springer's eBook collection, with millions of users worldwide. In addition, Briefs will be available for individual print and electronic purchase. Briefs are characterized by fast, global electronic dissemination, standard publishing contracts, easy-to-use manuscript preparation and formatting guidelines, and expedited production schedules. We aim for publication 8–12 weeks after acceptance. Both solicited and unsolicited manuscripts are considered for publication in this series.

**Indexing: This series is indexed in Scopus, Ei-Compendex, and zbMATH **

Jan Gogoll • Niina Zuber

Introduction to Ethical Software Development

 Springer

Jan Gogoll
Bayerisches Forschungsinstitut für Digitale
Transformation
München, Germany

Niina Zuber
Bayerisches Forschungsinstitut für Digitale
Transformation
München, Germany

ISSN 2191-5768   ISSN 2191-5776 (electronic)
SpringerBriefs in Computer Science
ISBN 978-3-032-06194-2   ISBN 978-3-032-06195-9 (eBook)
https://doi.org/10.1007/978-3-032-06195-9

This work was supported by Bayerisches Forschungsinstitut für Digitale Transformation.

© The Editor(s) (if applicable) and The Author(s) 2026. This book is an open access publication.
Open Access   This book is licensed under the terms of the Creative Commons Attribution 4.0 International License (http://creativecommons.org/licenses/by/4.0/), which permits use, sharing, adaptation, distribution and reproduction in any medium or format, as long as you give appropriate credit to the original author(s) and the source, provide a link to the Creative Commons license and indicate if changes were made.
The images or other third party material in this book are included in the book's Creative Commons license, unless indicated otherwise in a credit line to the material. If material is not included in the book's Creative Commons license and your intended use is not permitted by statutory regulation or exceeds the permitted use, you will need to obtain permission directly from the copyright holder.
The use of general descriptive names, registered names, trademarks, service marks, etc. in this publication does not imply, even in the absence of a specific statement, that such names are exempt from the relevant protective laws and regulations and therefore free for general use.
The publisher, the authors and the editors are safe to assume that the advice and information in this book are believed to be true and accurate at the date of publication. Neither the publisher nor the authors or the editors give a warranty, expressed or implied, with respect to the material contained herein or for any errors or omissions that may have been made. The publisher remains neutral with regard to jurisdictional claims in published maps and institutional affiliations.

This Springer imprint is published by the registered company Springer Nature Switzerland AG
The registered company address is: Gewerbestrasse 11, 6330 Cham, Switzerland

If disposing of this product, please recycle the paper.

To Viktoria and Romy
&
To Carsten, Julius and Jonna

Foreword

Digital technologies are reshaping our societies at a breathtaking pace. At the center of this transformation lies software: it drives our communication systems, infrastructures, decision-making tools, and, increasingly, even our moral landscapes. Yet, despite its profound societal relevance, the development of software systems has long proceeded without a robust and systematic integration of ethical reflection. It is here that the research project *Ethics in Agile Software Development* (EDAP) finds its motivation.

Launched in 2020 at the Bavarian Institute for Digital Transformation (bidt) in Munich, EDAP set out to explore a deceptively simple but deeply challenging question: *How can software be developed in an ethically adequate manner?* The project brought together perspectives from computer science, economics, and philosophy, as well as insights from real-world software development practice. Its goal was to design an approach that allows ethical questions to be detected, reflected upon, and translated into concrete technical requirements within agile development processes without disrupting the speed, flexibility, and iterative nature that make methods like Scrum so attractive.

At the heart of the project was the conviction that ethical deliberation must not be relegated to the periphery of development—to the kickoff phase or to ex-post assessments—but should instead accompany the entire lifecycle of software design and implementation. Ethical concerns arise in small, context-sensitive ways and at multiple decision points; they cannot be addressed solely through standardized checklists or post hoc evaluations. They require attentiveness, sensitivity to context, and the ability to weigh competing values—skills that must be supported and practiced within development teams.

This book is the intellectual culmination of the EDAP project co-authored by Dr. Niina Zuber and Dr. Jan Gogoll. It brings together 5 years of interdisciplinary collaboration and conceptual exploration. The book aims to bridge the gap between ethical theory and software practice. It introduces foundational concepts in digital ethics, highlights the distinctive nature of software as a technology, and offers a systematic approach to integrating ethics into the development process. This book aims to offer practitioners a clear orientation in the increasingly bewildering landscape of normative demands, value lists, ethical guidelines, and codes of conduct that have emerged around ethically informed software development. It speaks not only to philosophers and computer scientists but especially to practitioners, product managers, policymakers, and students who wish to understand the ethical dimensions of the software systems they develop or regulate.

We are pleased to see the outcomes of EDAP take shape in this form. The book reflects not only the authors' scholarly rigor but also their deep engagement with the practical challenges of ethical software development. It makes a valuable contribution to an emerging field that urgently needs thoughtful guidance, and we hope it will serve as a touchstone for further research, teaching, and reflection in this area.

We thank the Bavarian State Ministry for Science and the Arts and the Bavarian Research Institute for Digital Transformation (bidt) for their generous support of this project. We also extend our gratitude to the entire interdisciplinary team that made this work possible.

Technical University of Munich Alexander Pretschner
Bayerisches Forschungsinstitut für
Digitale Transformation
Munich, Germany

Ludwig-Maximilians-Universität München Julian Nida-Rümelin
Bayerisches Forschungsinstitut für
Digitale Transformation
Munich, Germany

Acknowledgment

We would like to express our deepest gratitude to the Bavarian Research Institute for Digital Transformation (bidt), an institute of the Bavarian Academy of Sciences and Humanities, for granting us the opportunity to pursue our research interests within the project "Ethical Deliberation for Agile Software Development" and for funding this endeavor. This book is the outcome of our collaborative deliberations and serves as a condensed reflection of our findings.

We are sincerely thankful to Alexander Pretschner and Julian Nida-Rümelin for their invaluable feedback, insightful thoughts, and continuous guidance throughout the past 5 years. We also wish to extend our thanks to our colleague, Severin Kacianka, whose expertise in software systems and development greatly enriched our thinking about the nature and necessity of ethical knowledge in this domain.

This research project is funded by the Bavarian Research Institute for Digital Transformation (bidt), an institute of the Bavarian Academy of Sciences and Humanities.

Competing Interests The authors have no competing interests to declare that are relevant to the content of this manuscript.

Contents

1	**Introduction**...		1
	References...		9
2	**What Is (Digital) Technology?**		11
	2.1	Different Perspectives on Technology	13
		2.1.1 How to Look at (Digital) Technology	14
		2.1.2 The Instrumental Perspective.........................	15
		2.1.3 The Transformative or Mediation Perspective...........	17
		2.1.4 The Contextual Perspective	18
		2.1.5 Conclusion: Three Perspectives on Ethics in Software Engineering	19
	2.2	The Uniqueness of Software	20
		2.2.1 The Relative Triviality of Manufacturing and Distribution	20
		2.2.2 Data Dependence....................................	21
		2.2.3 Engaging Reason and Simulating Emotions	22
		2.2.4 The Malleability of Software.........................	22
		2.2.5 The Imperceptible Nature of Software	24
		2.2.6 Persuasive Computing and the Ethical Challenge of Influence...	24
		2.2.7 Social Power of Software............................	25
		2.2.8 Diffusion of Responsibility	25
	References...		26
3	**Why Develop Software Ethically?**		29
	3.1	Why Anticipatory or Proactive Ethics?	31
	3.2	The Moral Responsibility of Software Production Companies....	33
	3.3	The Responsibility of Software Creators.....................	35

		3.4	Approaches to Ethical Software Development	38
			3.4.1 Principle-Based and Bottom-Up Approaches	38
			3.4.2 Why a Discursive Ethical Approach?	40
		3.5	Conclusion	41
		References		42
4	**What Is Ethics?**			**45**
	4.1	Ethics as a Science		47
		4.1.1	Consequentialism	49
		4.1.2	Deontology	50
		4.1.3	Virtue Ethics	51
		4.1.4	Contractualist Ethics	52
	4.2	From Applied Ethics to Domain Ethics		54
		4.2.1	Applied Ethics	56
		4.2.2	Domain-Specific Ethics	56
	4.3	Conclusion		58
	References			59
5	**Values and Software**			**61**
	5.1	Why Values Matter in Software Ethics		61
	5.2	Defining Values: Philosophical and Practical Dimensions		64
	5.3	Challenges of the Values Approach		66
	5.4	Values Provide Orientation: Values as an Epistemic Tool		68
	5.5	Two Kinds of Values: Techno-Generic and Domain-Specific		70
	5.6	Values in Conflict		72
	5.7	The Ethically Informed Triad: From Normative Analysis to the Technical Implementation of Value-Oriented Information Systems		74
	References			75
6	**Spotting the Right: Overcoming Moral Uncertainty**			**77**
	6.1	When Does a Question Stop Being Technical and Start Being Ethical? A Case for Ethics?		79
	6.2	Epistemia: Knowing What to Look at and What to Look for		81
	6.3	Who Needs to Be Part of the Ethical Discourse?		82
	6.4	Designing for the Mountains: Ethical Development of Avalanche Safety Apps		83
		6.4.1	Domain Knowledge	84
		6.4.2	Technology Expert	87
		6.4.3	Rights and Standards	91
		6.4.4	Domain Ethics	92
		6.4.5	Ethical Theories as Value Identification Method	96
		6.4.6	Stakeholders	96
	6.5	Avalanche Apps as a Case for Ethics		97
	References			99

7 Deciding for the Good: Overcoming Moral Indecisiveness ... 101
7.1 Deliberate Decisiveness ... 102
7.2 Why Value Ambiguity Is Inevitable ... 103
7.3 Ethical Deliberation in Software Design ... 104
7.4 Deliberative Decision-Making Phase: Navigating Ethical Disagreement ... 105
    7.4.1 A Balancing Game and the Search for Coherence ... 107
    7.4.2 Judging for the Good ... 108
    7.4.3 Software Engineering: Empowerment Through Participation ... 109
    7.4.4 Discursive Approach: Judging Together ... 110
    7.4.5 Ethical Dialogue in Teams ... 112
References ... 113

8 Organization, People and Processes ... 115
8.1 The Essential Role of (Organizational) Structure ... 117
    8.1.1 Ethical Software Development as an Organizational Endeavor ... 119
    8.1.2 Intra-, Inter-, and Organizational Level ... 120
8.2 Leveraging Agile Frameworks for Ethical Deliberation ... 125
    8.2.1 Mapping Agile to Ethical Deliberation ... 127
    8.2.2 Sprint 0: Unofficial but Essential for Ethical Deliberation ... 127
    8.2.3 Product Owner: Orchestrating Ethical Deliberation ... 130
References ... 132

Chapter 1
Introduction

Abstract This introductory chapter traces the historical arc from early automation to modern software, illustrating how technologies—initially designed as mere tools—have come to shape the very fabric of human life. Through the story of the Jacquard loom and its influence on computing, it explores how even modest design innovations can lead to far-reaching societal transformations. The chapter situates software as a distinct and paradigmatic form of technology, highlighting its ubiquity, opacity, and ethical significance. It argues that while software systems enable progress and efficiency, they also carry the power to reshape behaviors, social structures, and values—often invisibly. Ethical challenges in software development are rarely the result of malice; they stem more often from epistemic limitations or complex trade-offs. Drawing on real-world examples, the chapter makes the case for integrating ethical reflection into development processes from the outset. Rather than focusing only on harm prevention, it calls for a broader perspective that includes the cultivation of ethical excellence.

In the early 1800s, in the bustling workshops of Lyon, France, a revolutionary machine was making waves. It was the brainchild of Joseph Marie Jacquard, a weaver's son who, like many of his generation, wanted to simplify the complex process of weaving intricate patterns into fabric. Weaving, at the time, required skilled hands, long hours, and endless patience. Each delicate design meant painstakingly lifting specific threads by hand to create intricate patterns—a process that often took weeks to perfect. Jacquard had a different idea. Inspired by earlier innovations, he sought to automate weaving altogether. His invention, the Jacquard loom, was a remarkable feat of engineering. At the heart of this loom was a system of punched cards that controlled the pattern being woven into the fabric. Each card had a series of holes that directed the loom to lift specific threads, allowing it to create intricate patterns automatically, without the need for a human weaver to manually guide every step. In a metaphorical sense, Jacquard's loom could remember the pattern, as the punch cards stored the sequence for each unique design. This innovation radically transformed the textile industry, making it possible to mass-produce even the most elaborate fabrics. The Jacquard loom was a marvel of its time, blending craftsmanship with early forms of automation. Yet what no one could have

© The Author(s) 2026
J. Gogoll, N. Zuber, *Introduction to Ethical Software Development*,
SpringerBriefs in Computer Science,
https://doi.org/10.1007/978-3-032-06195-9_1

predicted was that this simple use of punched cards to control a weaving machine would eventually inspire a breakthrough in a completely different field: information technology. That this mechanical innovation would one day foreshadow the architecture of modern computers was, at the time, unimaginable. But not for everyone. Ada Lovelace, working with Charles Babbage on the design of the Analytical Engine, recognized the loom's deeper significance. In 1843, she observed that the machine could "weave algebraic patterns just as the Jacquard loom weaves flowers and leaves" (Lovelace, 1843), foreseeing that symbolic operations—not just textiles—could be automated. Her insight marks one of the first moments where the abstract power of computation was envisioned, long before its material realization.

Fast forward to the late nineteenth century, when the US Census Bureau faced an enormous challenge. The population was growing rapidly, and the traditional methods of counting people by hand were becoming unsustainable. It was a problem that demanded innovation. Enter Herman Hollerith, a young engineer who, like Jacquard, was searching for a way to simplify a complex process. Hollerith's idea? To take the punched card system used in the Jacquard loom and apply it to data. Much like Jacquard's loom used punched cards to store weaving patterns, Hollerith realized that punched cards could store information about people—age, gender, occupation, etc.—and then be fed into machines to process that data (this interestingly sounds very modern looking back even from 2025). His punch card system worked so efficiently that it cut the time to complete the 1890 census from nearly 10 years to just 2. What had once been a manual, labor-intensive process became a matter of feeding cards into a machine. This same punched card system became the foundation of early data processing, setting the stage for the computing revolution that would follow (and also why this book exists). It is almost poetic how the punch cards that once controlled the warp and weft of fabric would later control the flow of information in the emerging digital world. The intricate patterns they once helped create in silk and wool transformed into patterns of data—ones and zeros—that would shape the information age. This transformation is of such historical magnitude that it stands alongside, and arguably even surpasses, the invention of the printing press and the steam engine in its impact on human civilization. As computers advanced in the twentieth century, punch cards became indispensable in fields as diverse as government, business, and science. Programmers wrote code by punching holes into these cards, each card a line of instructions fed into the earliest computers. Entire systems, from payrolls to inventory, relied on them. What began with the goal of automating weaving and creating beautiful patterns more efficiently ended up becoming the foundation of modern information technology. The journey from Jacquard's loom to the first computers may seem like an unlikely one, but it reveals something fundamental: technology often grows in unexpected ways. The same principles that allowed a machine to weave fabric automatically eventually helped machines process and store vast amounts of data. The punch cards that revolutionized weaving went on to revolutionize the digital world, paving the way for modern society—including decent movie recommendations on Netflix and dates arranged via Tinder.

Yet as we look back on this transformation, it's worth asking: what happens when technology, created as a mere tool to simplify and serve, becomes integral to how we live and make decisions? The story of punch cards is not just one of innovation—it is also a reflection on responsibility. It prompts us to consider the role we want technology to play and the context in which it operates—in essence, what technology should be and how it ought to be designed. Today, as we build increasingly sophisticated systems, from algorithmic software to artificial intelligence, we must remember that the tools we create inevitably shape our world. And with that power comes the need for careful ethical consideration. Just as punch cards laid the foundation for the digital age, so too should we lay a foundation for ethical software engineering—one that recognizes both the potential and the responsibility that comes with building the systems of the future. This book is but a small part of this endeavor.

Technology has long been a main driver of profound changes in human society and life in general. However, as the title of this book suggests, our focus here will be specifically on software. Software is a unique form of technology that, as we will explore, differs in critical ways from other technological advancements. In many respects, it represents a paradigm shift, reshaping not only how we interact with the world but also how we think about ethics, responsibility, and societal impact. Software is not just *eating the world*, as Marc Andreessen famously put it: it's cooking, seasoning, and serving it up on a platter. In every corner of our lives, from the cars we drive to the news we consume, software is the unseen chef in the kitchen, shaping our daily experiences. But as it takes on this central role, the question of how we ethically *prepare* this digital feast becomes more crucial than ever. Just as a great meal can nourish and delight while a poorly made one with bad ingredients can lead to unpleasant outcomes, poorly crafted software can have unintended consequences, influencing our thoughts and behaviors and even our societies in ways we may not immediately realize. Of course, and quite obviously, well-designed software brings great benefits to both users and society as a whole. Just as a chef must consider the health and well-being of those who consume their food, an analogy can be drawn to software developers, who might also think about the broader impact of their creations. To finally bring this analogy to its inevitable—and frankly overdue—conclusion: it's not enough for a dish to merely provide sustenance; it should also be crafted with care, taking into account the quality of ingredients, the harmony of flavors, and its overall nutritional value. That said, and to preempt common objections, considerations of cost and time are both legitimate and necessary. Context always matters: a fast-food chain optimizes its offerings under entirely different constraints than a haute cuisine restaurant. In the same vein (this analogy, admittedly, continues to deliver), software development takes place across diverse environments with varying goals and limitations. While it is important to advocate for software that not only functions effectively but also reflects ethical considerations and contributes positively to human lives, such ambitions must be aligned with the specific context and purpose of the system being developed.

This book, *Introduction to Ethical Software Development*, aims to explore this crucial intersection of technology and ethics from an engineering point of view, that is, from the perspective of the producer. To grasp why a book on ethical software development is essential, we need to recognize that software occupies a unique and pivotal place in modern human life. And when we refer to software in this book, we mean explicitly all software, not just AI, despite what the current public discourse might suggest. Perhaps it is because AI acts like a magnifying glass, making underlying ethical issues more salient, which has brought these problems to the public's attention and garnered so much attention. Nevertheless, ethical questions in software development have existed long before the emergence of AI. In fact, many software engineers might be surprised that the current ethics debate is so heavily focused on AI, while broader software development is largely overlooked. While AI does present specific ethical challenges, the method of implementation—whether algorithmic or data-driven—ultimately seems to be of secondary importance when it comes to embedding ethical values and to create normatively aligned software products. Although it is obvious that different considerations must be made for each approach—whether a complex algorithm in a distributed system is genuinely less at risk of producing an ethically unwanted outcome or if it is always more transparent than a learned decision tree or neural network is at the very least debatable. This is why in this book, we aim to explore how ethical values can be generally incorporated into software development, with AI being just one, albeit significant, subfield. At times, we will take an even more abstract approach, treating software as a representation of technology as a whole. We take this approach because abstractions, once understood, offer the benefit of being adaptable across a range of unique contexts—a quality inherent to software itself. Additionally, software use is invariably linked to some form of hardware. While this book's focus clearly lies on software, it is helpful to remember that technology often represents more than just the sum of its parts.

It is beyond question that software is now ubiquitous in everyday life: it recommends movies, determines which news we see, controls cars, matches lovers, and calculates creditworthiness. Software also manages the routing of Internet traffic across the globe, optimizes supply chains for businesses, processes millions of financial transactions in real time, and powers search engines that index and retrieve vast amounts of information. Classical algorithms, often operating in distributed systems, are the backbone of these operations, ensuring efficiency, reliability, and speed in our digital interactions. In the case of generative artificial intelligence and large language models in particular, the output is even presented in the form of natural language, which gives the impression that it is based on intelligent, wise, or creative considerations (Zuber & Gogoll, 2024). However, the algorithms behind it largely remain hidden, with their workings opaque to the (every day) user and often even its creators. Software is often not directly or easily noticeable: we don't see it, hear it, or feel it. Typically, software systems function so seamlessly precisely because they require no explicit input. Our behavior serves as the input—often without our awareness that we're being used as data points. Unlike other technical objects, software operates in the hidden realm of cyberspace. We perceive the car, but not necessarily the computer that is built into it (ubiquitous computing). AI remains incomprehensible in its functioning as neural networks (non-explainability).

1 Introduction

We trust invisible and intangible software when we park a car or when doctors initiate therapy based on prognostic diagnostic tools. We communicate on social platforms, thereby altering the public sphere. For these reasons, software systems have such a profound impact on our way of life. Already this impact makes them ethically and morally significant. On one hand, they reinforce or change our interpersonal or societal demands, making them a topic of ethics. On the other hand, they can restrict individual freedoms, which is why they need to be morally evaluated.

It is not surprising, then, that demands for moral machines are becoming louder and more determined in casual conversations, talk shows, editorial pages, and scientific articles. This outcry stems from the implicit understanding that digital transformation should not have to be a form of *digital determinism* to which humanity must passively submit. Rather, it is a process shaped by human actors who have the power to actively guide it. It is not an inevitable fate to be accepted but a domain of intentional human agency and creation. Technology is inherently ambivalent. To illustrate this, consider two opposing extremes (exaggerated for clarity): On one side, we find the camp of what we would sometimes summarize as *technological optimists* or *techno-utopians* because they believe that technology can solve all problems and see it as the ultimate solution to societal, environmental, or personal challenges that humanity faces. Some might even be called *solutionists*, especially if they assume that complex human and societal problems can be reduced to technical solutions. On the opposite side, there is a form of *Neo-Luddism*, a perspective that critically opposes technological advancements, often viewing them as harmful to society, culture, or the environment. The Luddites were a group of English textile workers in the nineteenth century who resisted the introduction of certain automated machinery and organized raids to destroy the machines. Notably, it is no coincidence that the emergence of this movement coincides—both temporally and thematically—with the introduction of the Jacquard loom, which we discussed above.

In reality, most people do not fit neatly into either extreme but instead hold varied opinions depending on context and type of technology. For instance, someone might adopt a techno-optimist view by endorsing carbon-capture technology as the primary solution to combat climate change while disregarding the importance of behavioral changes. At the same time, they could express skepticism about dating apps with algorithmic matching, arguing that these threaten the authenticity of romantic relationships and should be approached cautiously. This would be a logically consistent position and thus unproblematic.

The debate between these two extremes is especially relevant when we consider the so-called Collingridge dilemma. The Collingridge dilemma, named after British philosopher David Collingridge, is a critical concept in the field of technology ethics. It highlights the challenges associated with controlling the development and impact of emerging technologies, e.g., software. The dilemma is twofold: on one hand, when a technology is in its early stages, its impacts are not well understood, making it difficult to predict and manage potential risks. On the other hand, once the technology has become well established and its effects are more apparent, it is often too late or too costly to change its course or mitigate its negative consequences. It describes the shift from a high-control, low-knowledge state to one of low control, high knowledge. This dilemma is particularly relevant in the context of digital technology and software development. As software systems become increasingly complex and embedded in every aspect of society, the difficulty of foreseeing their long-term impacts grows. The classic example is social networks. Early in the development process, software developers may not fully grasp the ethical implications of their designs or the potential for harm, whether it be in terms of privacy, security, or societal disruption. However, by the time these impacts become clear, the software may be so widespread and integrated into daily life that reversing or altering it would be extremely challenging. This concept is tied to the well-known idea of *die normative Kraft des Faktischen* by Georg Jellinek (1900/2013), which can be roughly translated from its original German as *The normative force of the factual*. Jellinek introduced this idea in his work on legal theory in 1900, highlighting how established facts or realities often shape norms and influence what is considered acceptable or right even if they were initially unintended or undesired.

This underscores the importance of integrating ethical considerations early and consistently in the software development lifecycle—as a proactive approach. In this book, we will delve into the epistemic challenges of ethical software engineering, with the aim of raising the reader's awareness and providing the tools to hopefully equip them to identify ethical issues early on and act appropriately.

In exploring ethical software development, it is helpful to remember that concrete examples often bridge understanding. Take, for instance, the case of New York's low-hanging bridges, discussed in Langdon Winner's (1980) seminal article, "Do Artifacts Have Politics?", which is often referenced to illustrate potential impact of so-called *neutral* technology. These bridges, designed under the direction of Robert Moses, were intentionally built low to restrict access for public buses, which predominantly served lower-income communities and people of color, thus limiting their ability to access certain recreational areas. This physical design decision, seemingly technical, had profound social implications, reflecting how technological choices can embody and perpetuate societal values and biases. In other cases, there may be unintended consequences that result out of seemingly neutral design choices and business, influencing user behavior and societal outcomes. A modern example is found in music streaming platforms (Hesmondhalgh, 2022): because artists are paid only if listeners reach a certain threshold, songs have evolved to grab attention instantly—often sacrificing the long, expressive intros once typical in music like Led Zeppelin's "Stairway to Heaven." This shift reveals how software can shape not only industries but also art forms and individual creativity, underscoring the ethical implications of design choices in today's digital age. Note that these impacts may not stem from malicious intent but could simply result from a lack of awareness—a pattern we believe lies at the heart of most ethically problematic software implementations and one that we hope this book can help mitigate, even if just a little.

Therefore, it's crucial to recognize that not all cases are created equal and ethical issues in software development exist in varied forms. Broadly, ethical challenges can stem from deliberate wrongdoing or from unforeseen consequences of seemingly neutral design decisions. This distinction is important, as it impacts how we address and learn from these issues. For example, consider the Volkswagen (VW) emissions scandal, where engineers deliberately programmed diesel engines to meet emissions standards only under testing conditions, knowing the vehicles would emit far higher pollutants during normal driving. This was a calculated decision, made to deceive regulators and consumers—an ethical breach so clear-cut that it leaves no room for debate about the morality of the action. This book is not aimed at those who engage in overt fraud, as there is no ethical ambiguity to explore in such cases. Deliberate deception goes against fundamental ethical principles and falls outside the scope of constructive ethical discussion for responsible software development. We believe that most ethically relevant issues in software development do not fall into the category of outright deception. In fact, if they did, there would be little reason for this book. Rather than assuming that people are inherently dishonest on a large scale, we take a practical approach, recognizing that engineers and management often find themselves in challenging situations. These challenges stem from constraints such as limited resources, tight timelines, gaps in knowledge, organizational structures that may hinder ethical decision-making, and incentives that can unintentionally misalign with ethical goals. We try to bring these factors into the spotlight.

In contrast to the case of deception at VW, other ethical issues in technology are more complex and, in some cases, were unanticipated. Take the example of social media, where platforms designed initially to connect people and share information have inadvertently facilitated the rapid spread of misinformation and "fake news." When social media platforms emerged, it may not have been obvious that the algorithms optimizing for engagement would create echo chambers, amplifying misinformation and impacting public opinion and even democratic processes. Similarly, Amazon's hiring algorithm, intended to automate and improve the hiring process, was found to be biased against women—a consequence of training data reflecting historical gender imbalances in certain job roles. These instances highlight how ethical issues can arise unintentionally, stemming from design choices that, while technically sound, carry unanticipated societal impacts.

This book aims to address these nuanced ethical concerns—where the intent is not to deceive but where design choices lead to broader consequences that developers may not have fully anticipated. By understanding these complex cases, developers can better recognize and mitigate ethical risks, fostering a more conscientious approach to software development. The examples above highlight that ethical issues aren't always easy to identify in advance or during the development process. This book, therefore, seeks to equip readers with tools to better anticipate ethical concerns before products are launched or resources are invested. For instance, Amazon's hiring algorithm, which was ultimately scrapped due to its bias against women, was discovered to have issues before release but only after substantial time and resources had already been invested. This case underscores an epistemic challenge, where problems emerge late in development due to gaps in knowledge or understanding. The social media and misinformation issue, on the other hand, presents a different challenge due to its layered complexity. Philosopher Shannon Vallor (2016) aptly questions in her book, *Technology and the Virtues*, "Is Twitter good?" pointing out that such a question is overly simplistic. While fake news is inherently concerning, determining what qualifies as "fake" is often nuanced, and this decision can be contentious. Similarly, while an unfairly biased hiring algorithm is undesirable, we must not forget that an algorithm's purpose is inherently to discriminate in the original meaning of the word—to make decisions based on set criteria is its very reason for existence. A hiring tool that doesn't discern at all would be ineffective and pointless, but the ethical challenge arises when that discernment becomes unjust. And the little word "unjust" carries all the weight here.

Often, ethical considerations involve balancing legitimate values that conflict. Consider Apple's practice of throttling iPhone performance for older batteries also known as *Batterygate*. Critics argue this incentivizes customers to buy new phones as an instance of planned obsolescence, while Apple claims it's intended to protect battery health and extend the device's lifespan. No matter which perspective one finds more compelling, the ethical boundaries are less clear than in cases like VW's deliberate deception or Amazon's (unintendedly biased) hiring algorithm. This book aims to address these subtle, complex ethical questions, where arguments based on ethical values might point in different directions, helping developers navigate these gray areas in responsible and informed ways (Chap. 4).

As you can see, we have so far focused primarily on negative cases—situations that are typically considered blameworthy. This is not incidental. In both philosophical literature and everyday discourse, blame tends to receive far more attention than praise. It reflects a broader tendency, captured by the old adage: bad news travels fast. One reason is that blameworthiness is often linked to liability—to sanctions, consequences, or corrective action—making it appear more urgent than praiseworthiness. As philosopher Gary Watson points out, we even have a richer vocabulary for expressing blame than for praise: it feels natural to say someone is *to blame* for a failure, but it feels a little awkward to say someone is *to be praised* for a success. Even phrases like *holding someone responsible* typically arise in contexts of fault or harm. Moreover, while small moral failings may draw criticism, merely doing what is right—being minimally decent—rarely earns recognition (Talbert, 2024). This asymmetry may be understandable, but it is also limiting. If we are serious about fostering a responsible culture in software development, then our attention must go beyond preventing harm. We must also cultivate and recognize ethical excellence—celebrating those who make thoughtful, principled choices even in the absence of crisis.

What emerges from all of this is clear: ethical software development is not a marginal concern—it is central to the future of responsible innovation. But how can software producers navigate this increasingly complex terrain? How do ethical principles translate into practice, and what tools can help identify, evaluate, and implement them in real-world projects? These are the questions this book sets out to explore. The chapters that follow are designed to offer both conceptual clarity and practical guidance. Each one builds toward a deeper understanding of how ethical software development can become a lived reality.

References

Hesmondhalgh, D. (2022). Streaming's effects on music culture: Old anxieties and new simplifications. *Cultural Sociology, 16*(1), 3–24.

Jellinek, G., & Jellinek, W. (1900/2013). *Allgemeine Staatslehre: Manuldruck*. Springer-Verlag.

Lovelace, A. (1843). Notes by the translator. *Scientific Memoirs, III*, 691–731.

Talbert, M. (2024). Moral responsibility. In E. N. Zalta & U. Nodelman (Eds.), *The Stanford encyclopedia of philosophy*. Retrieved from https://plato.stanford.edu/archives/fall2024/entries/moral-responsibility

Vallor, S. (2016). *Technology and the virtues: A philosophical guide to a future worth wanting*. Oxford University Press.

Winner, L. (1980). Do artifacts have politics? *Daedalus, 109*(1), 121–136.

Zuber, N., & Gogoll, J. (2024). Vox populi, vox ChatGPT: Large language models, education and democracy. *Philosophies, 9*(1), 13.

Open Access This chapter is licensed under the terms of the Creative Commons Attribution 4.0 International License (http://creativecommons.org/licenses/by/4.0/), which permits use, sharing, adaptation, distribution and reproduction in any medium or format, as long as you give appropriate credit to the original author(s) and the source, provide a link to the Creative Commons license and indicate if changes were made.

The images or other third party material in this chapter are included in the chapter's Creative Commons license, unless indicated otherwise in a credit line to the material. If material is not included in the chapter's Creative Commons license and your intended use is not permitted by statutory regulation or exceeds the permitted use, you will need to obtain permission directly from the copyright holder.

Chapter 2
What Is (Digital) Technology?

> "Technology is a mode of revealing. Technology comes to presence in the realm where revealing and unconcealment take place, where aletheia, truth, happens"
>
> Martin Heidegger, The Question Concerning Technology

Abstract Technology profoundly shapes human life, influencing how we live, work, and understand the world. This chapter explores various philosophical perspectives on technology, highlighting instrumental, mediation, and pragmatic perspectives. The instrumental perspective regards technology as a neutral tool whose ethical implications depend solely on human use. In contrast, the mediation perspective argues that technology actively shapes human perceptions, experiences, and interactions, embedding inherent normative influences within its very structure. The pragmatic or contextual perspective expands this discussion by illustrating how technology reshapes societal norms and practices, affecting fundamental aspects of social systems such as communication and urban planning. Significantly, digital technologies—and software in particular—stand out as a unique form of technology, prompting the need for specialized ethical considerations. Unlike traditional physical technologies, software is characterized by ease of replication, rapid scalability, pervasive invisibility, and the capacity to mediate complex human experiences and decisions. By analyzing these distinct features and their ethical implications, the chapter underscores that software producers carry a significant ethical responsibility. They are not merely creators of neutral tools but stewards of technology that profoundly mediates and shapes human life and social structures.

Humanity's relationship with technology is not a recent development (although it has probably become more important and definitely more salient); it has been an integral part of our existence since the dawn of time. In Greek mythology, the titan Prometheus stole fire from the gods, gave it to the humans, and suffered eternal punishment for his defiance. And just as if inspired by Prometheus, we humans have pursued technology as a force of transformation—something that promises power, progress, and a release from our limitations. Fire, in this sense, was the first technology, illuminating the world but also capable of destruction. This echoes today's discussions around AI, where some would argue that existential risks stand side by side with undeniable benefits. Technology, from the earliest stone tools to the advent of the wheel, and now to the age of AI, has continuously evolved alongside us, driving progress and shaping civilizations—sometimes in ways we barely notice, other times in ways we cannot ignore. This interdependence has made technology a crucial force in defining human experience and potential and has triggered philosophical investigation from the beginning. Employing technology could almost be considered to be part of the *Conditio humana*, i.e., something that defines us as human and thus sets us apart from other lifeforms on the planet. Aristotle, for instance, viewed technology as an extension of nature, where human ingenuity and tools could enhance our natural capabilities. He distinguished between *techne*—the knowledge of making things, which includes both the practical skills and the principles behind them—and *episteme*, or theoretical knowledge. For Aristotle (2014), *techne* was essential in shaping the material world and advancing human society, demonstrating how deeply intertwined technology has always been with human development. Important for Aristotle was that the skills should fit a desirable human *praxis*. Skills and technologies, in Aristotle's view, should not merely serve practical goals in isolation but should fit into and enhance broader, meaningful human practices. The use of skills must contribute to the good life, one that reflects ethical principles and human flourishing. For instance, a craftsperson's skill is not valuable only for producing an object but for how the practice of craftsmanship reflects care and purpose and thus contributes to a larger societal good. Roughly two millennia later, during the Enlightenment, Immanuel Kant (Recki, 2021) emphasized the role of technology in human autonomy and moral development. He saw technological advancement as a means of exercising human reason and improving the human condition, aligning it with the Enlightenment ideal of progress. Kant believed that through the responsible use of technology, humanity could achieve greater freedom and mastery over the natural world, implicating the importance of ethical considerations in technological development. In the twentieth century, Martin Heidegger (1977) offered a more critical perspective on technology. He argued that modern technology had transformed from a mere tool into a force that shapes human existence, often in ways that distance us from our authentic selves. Heidegger warned that technology's dominance could lead to a standing-reserve mentality, where everything, including humans, is viewed as a resource to be optimized and exploited.

In any case, technology has undeniably had a profound impact on humanity. Consider the influence of artificial lighting on our daily activities and planning or the medieval invention of the stirrup, which is often credited with playing an important role to enable feudalism to become the dominant form of governance in Europe by allowing mounted knights to fight more effectively, thereby solidifying the power of the warrior class. Similarly, the widespread adoption of gunpowder centuries later played a significant role in the decline of feudalism by rendering traditional knightly combat and castle defenses obsolete, shifting military power to centralized states with professional armies or mercenaries. The printing press, invented by Johannes Gutenberg in the mid-fifteenth century, marked the beginning of the Information Age and the rise of mass media. By enabling the rapid and wide dissemination of knowledge, it revolutionized communication, making books, pamphlets, and other printed materials accessible to a much larger audience—challenging and reshaping the balance of power, as exemplified by the impact of the ideas of Martin Luther. Similarly, the watermill, a seemingly humble innovation, had a profound effect on medieval society. By greatly increasing the efficiency of grain processing, watermills contributed to agricultural surpluses, which supported population growth and the development of towns and trade. This technology not only eased the labor burden but also facilitated the expansion of economies, helping lay the foundation for the complex social and economic structures that followed. Fast-forwarding a few centuries (and to get closer to the focus of this book), the development of the Internet stands out as one of the most transformative impacts of software—reshaping everything from communication to commerce and connecting the world like never before. These examples illustrate how technological innovations, whether rather simple like the stirrup or much more complex like the Internet, have been pivotal in shaping the trajectory of human history, influencing everything from social structures to the flow of information and even how we understand ourselves as human beings. Why should you, the reader, care about these historical examples? First, they demonstrate the profound impact technology can have on humanity, emphasizing the importance of reflecting on this fact if you are involved in creating it. Second, as you'll see in the following discussion, our understanding of the nature of technology significantly influences where we assign responsibility. We will now discuss how we can understand the nature of technology.

2.1 Different Perspectives on Technology

Software has become an invisible yet pervasive force in our lives, shaping decisions about what we watch, where we go, and even how we are evaluated for credit. These systems often operate seamlessly, relying on our behavior as input without requiring explicit interaction. We provide data unknowingly, and in a way, we become the input. While this efficiency is a hallmark of modern technology, it also raises significant ethical concerns. The algorithms driving these systems are hidden, their mechanisms opaque, and their impacts profound, yet not always positive. This prompts pressing questions: How can we address the negative consequences of software systems? How can we foster desirable output? At what stage should interventions occur? Who bears the responsibility: the state, the company, the operator, the developer, or the user?

This chapter looks at how technology cannot always be perceived as a mere tool we use but also something that changes how we see the world and how we act in it. For example, consider navigation apps like Google Maps or Waze. In the past, people used physical maps and relied on their own judgment or asked others for directions, which created a sense of awareness about their surroundings and encouraged social interaction. Now, navigation apps have changed this completely. They do not just give directions; they also influence our choices about where to go, how to get there, and even what mode of travel to use. These apps show us a version of the world that is shaped by algorithms, focusing on speed and efficiency rather than exploration or spontaneity. As a result, our relationship with our environment has changed. Instead of discovering places naturally, we follow optimized routes, making us prioritize convenience over context or discovery. Even how we think about "navigating" has shifted. With features like real-time tracking and suggested routes, a simple walk might feel more like a guided tour, with apps steering us toward specific paths or landmarks. This can be described as the normative impact that technology exerts.

Evaluating software requires a distinct perspective, as it differs fundamentally from traditional tools like a hammer. Unlike simple, physical tools, software is a complex, dynamic system that interacts with its environment and users in intricate ways. It shapes human behavior, influences decision-making, and mediates social interactions, making it necessary to consider not only its functionality but also its broader impact. This is what we are going to discuss in this chapter. First, however, we are going to explore different perspectives on technology in general, and then we are going to shift our focus to software to examine what makes it unique and special.

2.1.1 How to Look at (Digital) Technology

A very basic definition of software would be that it consists of programs that run on hardware. Programs transform input data into output data. Some people see software as just another tool to make life easier or to help us achieve our goals. Others view it as something much more powerful: a technology that changes how we experience the world. The way we think about software, even if we do not realize it, affects how we approach its ethical implications. Consider again the example of a navigation app like Google Maps. On the surface, it might seem like a straightforward input-output system: users enter their destination (input) and receive a recommended route (output). However, this seemingly simple process is influenced by a wide range of complex factors, including real-time traffic data, user location history, and predictive algorithms that estimate travel time. The ethical implications arise when we consider how these inputs are processed.

Developers need to think not just about how their products are used but also about how they influence behavior and decision-making. By looking at software from both a practical and a deeper, transformational perspective, we can better connect ethical ideas with real-world challenges, giving us the tools to handle the complex issues that come with creating and using software.

From a **means-end perspective**, also known as the *instrumental view*, technology is seen as a tool created to achieve specific goals or fulfill certain needs. In this view, technology is simply a means to an end, serving as a neutral instrument that we use to accomplish tasks or solve problems, i.e., to use Google Maps to get to the movies.

The **transformative perspective**, also known as the *mediation perspective*, emphasizes that technology is more than a tool for practical use. It actively transforms human experiences, perceptions, and actions. Thus, technology is not neutral; it influences how we engage with the world and with each other, i.e., to look at Google Maps to find movie theaters. Through its design, technology conveys and perpetuates specific values, shaping behaviors and decisions.

The **contextual perspective** focuses on the shifts that technology brings to the fundamental cornerstones of social systems, features that define and differentiate areas of life such as work, education, or communication. These cornerstones are not just descriptive; they have an *ought-to* character, meaning they are essentially normative in nature. They shape what is considered appropriate, expected, or required within a particular domain. This perspective examines how technology touches these normative foundations, altering the structure of our social subsystems and the way we understand and engage with different aspects of life.

The instrumental, transformative, and contextual perspectives offer distinct ways of understanding technology's impact, each with implications for the responsibility of software engineers. From an instrumental perspective, the navigation app is a neutral tool designed to help users find efficient routes and destinations. Software engineers' responsibility, in this view, is straightforward: to ensure the app functions reliably and achieves its intended purpose. The transformative perspective, however, highlights how the app reshapes individual users' perceptions and actions, such as how they understand time, space, and convenience. Here, engineers must consider the app's influence on behavior, like encouraging reliance on algorithms over personal judgment or exploration. The contextual perspective broadens the scope further, examining how the app redefines societal norms or conventions such as reducing face-to-face interactions for directions or prioritizing efficiency over spontaneity in travel.

Together, these perspectives illustrate that software engineers are not just creators of tools but stewards of technology's broader societal effects, requiring them to address both immediate functionality and far-reaching ethical implications. Next, we will examine these perspectives in greater detail.

2.1.2 The Instrumental Perspective

Possibly due to its intuitive appeal, apparent plausibility, and the fact that instrumental considerations are often the motivation for creating technology, the instrumental perspective of technology is a prevalent prima facie viewpoint. It regards technology, including software, as a neutral tool that humans build and use to achieve various ends. The premise is that humans are the subjects and technology is an object. While subjects possess autonomy and intentions necessary to set specific ends, objects are inert and serve merely as a means to those ends. This perspective posits that technology itself does not possess intrinsic ethical values and is thus value neutral; rather, the ethical implications arise from how individuals choose to utilize any given (software) tool. Therefore, software itself is neither ethically good or bad; it is the people who use it for good or bad purposes or accidentally misuse it. An often-used analogy to illustrate this point is the metaphor of the hammer. A hammer, like software, is a form of technology, but it is more intuitively seen as a mere tool compared to, say, a machine learning algorithm. With a hammer, it is clear that you can use it for its intended purpose, such as driving a nail into a wall, or *misuse* it by physically harming someone. In this case, the outcome seems entirely dependent on the human intention and context of use, with the tool being rather incidental—it could just as easily have been a log. The analogy is then extended to more complex technologies: what is true for the hammer must also be true for other more complex technologies, even if understanding the context or intention is more complicated. Fundamentally, they are still used as mere value-neutral tools that can be (mis)used by a moral agent, yet the software, in and of itself, does not carry moral weight.

Consider the example of a software package used for data analysis, such as STATA, SPSS, or Python libraries like SciKit-Learn or NumPy: data analysis software and tools can be employed in beneficial ways, such as optimizing farming practices to increase crop yields, reduce waste, and promote sustainable farming methods. It can also enable predictive analytics to combat poaching in Africa, thereby preserving wildlife, which is widely regarded as positive. However, data analysis can also be used in morally undesirable or unacceptable ways, as seen in the Cambridge Analytica case, potentially undermining democratic institutions like elections (Susser et al., 2019). Additionally, predictive policing software could impose a dystopian and biased version of society if misused. The instrumental perspective asserts that it is the humans who use the tool, their intentions, and the context of its usage that make the use of an inherently value-neutral tool morally problematic—not something that is embodied in the artifact itself. The philosopher Sven Nyholm puts it elegantly:

> Accordingly, if bad things happen and technologies are involved, we should not blame the technologies, but the people who use them for their own ends, which might be morally problematic. On the flipside, when technologies are used for good ends, the instrumental theory implies that we should not thank or praise the technologies but the people who create or use them. (Nyholm, 2022)

It is clear why the perspective we adopt regarding the ethical nature of technology is crucial for our broader discussion of ethical software engineering. The instrumental perspective places most of the responsibility on the user of the software, leaving little to none on the producer (given the technology functions as intended). This shift in responsibility diminishes the importance of ethical software development. To foster morally good outcomes and prevent bad ones, a purely instrumental perspective primarily relies on two approaches: First, it places the burden on regulators to create laws and regulations that guide the proper use of the neutral tool to achieve good ends and avoid bad ones. Second, it emphasizes educating users to understand the technology, prevent misuse, and encourage them to pursue positive outcomes. The instrumental perspective is often implicitly prevalent among software engineers, as they see themselves as problem-solvers who provide tools to achieve specific ends. However, this view is often a naive variant of the instrumental perspective and frequently goes unexamined. When confronted with the strict instrumental perspective, people often sense that technology may involve more than just being a value-neutral tool.

2.1.3 The Transformative or Mediation Perspective

The transformative perspective on technology offers a nuanced understanding of how technology influences and shapes human experiences, perceptions, and interactions. In the literature, it is often called the mediation perspective. The word mediate comes from the Latin word *medius*, meaning middle, and mediators are positioned between parties. In the context of technology, this means that technologies stand between us and the world, interpreting the world for us in ways that go beyond the function of a mere tool. The mediation perspective thus acknowledges that technology plays an active role in our relationship with the world. Those who adhere to this perspective shift their focus from how humans use tools to how the technologies influence our perception of the world. This perspective thus proposes a transformation of the subject-world relationship through the use of technology and as such technology itself becomes somehow value laden. This is particularly significant if the user has no control over how their perception is being altered.

As Don Ihde (1990) explained, technology expands our knowledge and enriches how we interact with the world, making things more accessible and allowing us to interpret our environment differently. Sometimes, technology works quietly in the background to help us overcome limitations of our human physicality, the classic example being a central heating system that provides our bodies with the right room temperature often without us actively realizing that it exists because we do not actively interact with it (in contrast to a classic radiator that we actively adjust). Another important way we interact with technology is when it becomes like an extension of our body. Consider glasses, which change how we relate to the world by improving vision, or a powered exoskeleton that is connected to the human body and amplifies its strength. These examples are of the so-called embodiment relation we can have with technologies.

Other times, it becomes a tool that we actively use to understand more about our surroundings. One classic example of how technology mediates the way we perceive the world is the thermometer because it illustrates how technology mediates our perception and interpretation of the world in subtle yet profound ways. Prior to the invention of the thermometer, people assessed temperature subjectively, relying on their personal sensations of hot or cold. The thermometer introduced an objective, quantifiable measure of temperature, shifting our perception of thermal conditions from subjective experiences to objective data points. Unlike the instrumental perspective, which would view the thermometer merely as a tool for measuring temperature, the mediation perspective recognizes that the thermometer—in a way—transforms our relationship with the world, i.e., temperature. It changes how we perceive and interpret the environment. Consider the case of a fever: we now have precise definitions for when someone has a fever, including specific temperature thresholds that indicate when it begins and when it becomes dangerous. Before thermometers, doctors relied solely on their senses to determine if a patient was "hot," diagnosing a fever only in obvious cases and with some uncertainty. This makes it easier to grasp why Ihde calls this the hermeneutic relationship: it provides more information about the world that we need to interpret. Finally, we have something we may call alterity relations. These describe the way humans experience technologies as if they were others or entities with a degree of independence different from us. In these interactions, the technology presents itself as a quasi-other, engaging users in a way that resembles encountering another being. This can occur when technologies appear to act autonomously or respond to human actions in ways that suggest agency. For example, interacting with a voice assistant like Alexa or Siri or conversing with a large language model is a case of an alterity relation, but also less sophisticated technologies like an ATM machine could evoke these experiences. Users often perceive these systems as entities with which they can interact ("Why won't you [computer] just do what I'm telling you?!"), even though they are obviously not conscious beings. This relationship highlights how technologies can evoke a sense of otherness and blur the boundary between tools and independent agents.

If we understand technology as a mediator, it becomes clear why we cannot simply talk about its use as being purely desirable or valuable. Therefore, if we view technology as a mediating tool, it becomes clear that the design and structure of the tool itself are already significant. For example, take a washing machine: it is pre-programmed to determine how much water is optimal for washing regarding some specific understanding of optimality by the producer, and the user cannot easily change this setting, even if they might prefer to use less water for ecological reasons. This shows how technology shapes not only our perception but also our choices.

Of course, any technology can be analyzed both as a tool (a means to an end) and as a mediator (something that influences how we perceive and interact with the world). Importantly, when technology acts as a mediator, ethical responsibility shifts. It's not just about how we use the technology but also about how the design and built-in limitations and possibilities of the technology affect our actions and decisions.

2.1.4 The Contextual Perspective

The contextual perspective goes beyond the immediate effects of digital technology on individual users to explore its deeper impact on the underlying structures and norms that shape society. It focuses on how technology transforms the rules of the game—the foundational principles that define and differentiate various areas of life, such as work, education, governance, or communication. These foundational rules are inherently normative, carrying an *ought-to* character that guides how individuals and groups ought to behave within specific social domains (Nida-Rümelin, 2023).

For example, consider again a navigation app. From an instrumental perspective, these apps are tools designed to help users find efficient routes. From a mediation perspective, they reshape how individuals perceive space, time, and decision-making by relying on algorithms for directions rather than their judgment or exploration. But from a contextual perspective, navigation apps go even further: They redefine the broader societal norms around travel and spatial awareness. Before such apps, navigation often involved community interactions, like asking for directions or restaurant recommendations, which fostered a sense of local knowledge and social engagement. Now, the reliance on apps has diminished these interactions, altering the social fabric of how we navigate physical spaces.

On a larger scale, these apps influence urban planning by, e.g., prioritizing road efficiency for vehicles over pedestrian-friendly designs, and they reshape societal expectations about convenience and speed. The contextual perspective reveals how such technologies impact systemic structures: how we organize cities, how we value efficiency over exploration, and how we conceptualize our relationship with our environment by influencing, e.g., the normative boundaries that distinguish public traffic from off-road biking. By examining technology through this lens, the contextual perspective highlights how it transforms the very fabric of social life, creating new norms, dependencies, and power dynamics.

2.1.5 Conclusion: Three Perspectives on Ethics in Software Engineering

At this point, one may ask: how does this distinction advance the broader argument of the book on ethical software development? A main point that we will come back to in the next chapter is responsibility. When we recognize that technology does more than serve as a mere or neutral instrument—that it actively mediates how people perceive, experience, and interact with the world—the ethical spotlight shifts from how a tool is *used* to how it is *conceived* and *built*. Designers, engineers, and product teams are therefore not just tackling technical challenges; through the choices they embed in code and interfaces, they help configure the world their users encounter. That formative power is part of what grounds ethical responsibility on the production side of software.

However, while these perspectives highlight the broader ethical landscapes shaped by technology, it still lacks clear criteria for determining when these transformations cross the line into ethically problematic territory, leaving open the critical question of how to evaluate the moral consequences of these profound social shifts. Can we identify specific criteria in the upcoming discussion of uniqueness that would allow us to better define when these technological impacts become morally concerning? Or perhaps, should we expand our attentiveness to capture these nuances more effectively?

2.2 The Uniqueness of Software

At this point, it is important to address why ethical software development warrants specific attention. If software were merely another form of technology, one might simply write about "ethical technology production" more broadly and kill two birds with one stone. Of course, one could argue that software differs in many respects, including its cultural characteristics, e.g., the silicon valley inspired goals of innovation and progress or the geek culture of open source. While this may be true, we argue that software in and of itself is already a uniquely distinct form of technology, deserving of its own special attention and dedicated focus. In other words, software differs so significantly from fields like chemical or civil engineering that, upon reflection, it becomes clear that we must take steps to understand these differences and their ethical implications. As we delve deeper into the topic of information technology, it is evident that these digital artifacts possess unique characteristics that necessitate normative assessment. To address the ethics of software, we must identify the distinctive aspects that set digital technologies apart and narrow down the situations that arise decidedly due to their information technology character. This *uniqueness* is encapsulated in the adage: "We just replaced your entire industry with 100 lines of Python code." This saying highlights the transformative power of software to disrupt traditional industries with minimal code (of course relying on loads of already existing libraries), emphasizing the profound impact inherent in digital innovation but also the power and responsibility associated with it. But what makes software and information technologies so distinct? We argue that several key characteristics define their uniqueness, each with important ethical implications that will be explored in the following discussion. As this is a book on ethical software development, understanding these distinctive features is essential, as they also shed light on questions of responsibility, the consequences of actions and practical things we need to consider when building information technology systems.

2.2.1 The Relative Triviality of Manufacturing and Distribution

One of the most striking differences is that software lacks physical substance. Unlike physical products that require raw materials, manufacturing processes, and physical distribution networks, software can be produced, duplicated, and distributed with minimal effort and cost. The marginal cost of shipping out any additional piece of software over the Internet is virtually zero. This triviality in manufacturing and the low roll-out costs mean that software can be iterated upon far more rapidly than physical technologies. Arguably, due to coding agents such as Claude code, the manufacturing of software has recently taken another boost in productivity. Note, the term *triviality* is not meant to be degrading, i.e., that software development is easy, but rather highlights the comparative ease of these processes relative to other types of engineering. While manufacturing a car, a building, or a chemical compound involves significant physical effort, the replication and distribution of software are largely instantaneous and cost-effective. However, this ease of distribution also amplifies the potential impact of software—both positive and negative—at an unprecedented scale, making ethical considerations more critical.

These characteristics have an impact on how the production process is organized and conducted: the "measure twice, cut once" approach that defines many physical engineering disciplines *seems* far less relevant in software engineering. After all, bugs can be patched, features can be added, and entire systems can be redesigned even after deployment (albeit not without causing major headaches). While this flexibility is an obvious strength in many aspects, it also raises unique challenges. For instance, the ease of post-deployment changes can lead to rushed or careless development practices, knowing that issues can be addressed later. Beta testing serves as a striking example of the unique characteristics of information technology. This practice is entirely standard in software development. To illustrate the contrast, imagine a structural engineer asking you, the reader, to "beta-test" a newly constructed bridge by driving your car over it. Or to use a less safety-critical example, imagine beta-testing a new adhesive glue for envelopes that later prove ineffective under the rigors and stresses of postal handling, requiring the recall of tens of thousands of envelopes. The absurdity of such a scenario underscores just how different software can be from traditional engineering disciplines. To be fair, this is typically not an issue in highly regulated and safety-critical industries since regulations are in place that address this very issue. However, software is ubiquitous, and regulation cannot feasibly encompass the vast majority of software applications—leaving us with the task of developing *good* software anyway.

Another connected point is that software also differs in its capacity to scale. Watts Humphrey highlighted the stark contrast between the scales encountered in civil engineering versus software engineering. A civil engineer typically deals with structures whose dimensions vary by no more than two orders of magnitude, such as a house versus a skyscraper or a model of a bridge and the actual bridge. In contrast, software developers move from writing small programs of a few hundred lines of code in college to working on systems with millions of lines of code in the real world—a difference of three orders of magnitude. This massive scalability introduces complexities that are unique to software, such as maintaining functionality, performance, and security at a scale unimaginable in most physical engineering contexts.

2.2.2 Data Dependence

Unlike traditional technologies such as a hammer, a bicycle, or even an electric motor, software requires structured *input* to generate meaningful *output*, making it fundamentally *data driven*. While a bicycle operates the same regardless of who rides it, a navigation app like Google Maps dynamically adapts to user input, traffic data, and location history to generate route suggestions. This dependency on data creates unique ethical challenges, especially when the methods of data acquisition are opaque or invasive. For example, large-scale machine learning systems are often trained by scraping vast amounts of data from the Internet, including texts, images, and behavioral traces, frequently without the explicit knowledge or consent of the individuals involved. This practice raises profound concerns about privacy, autonomy, and digital consent, as it effectively turns online behavior into raw material for algorithmic processing. In contrast to physical technologies whose ethical implications are often tied to their use, software blurs the line between tool and observer, continuously collecting, interpreting, and acting upon personal data often invisibly and asymmetrically.

2.2.3 Engaging Reason and Simulating Emotions

Another aspect closely related to the medial and contextual perspective is that digital technologies no longer primarily enhance physical strength but instead influence thinking, communication, and emotions—fundamental aspects of what we consider to be uniquely human. Digital technologies increasingly extend beyond automating physical labor to becoming decision-supportive tools designed to perform intellectual and emotional tasks. These technologies engage with phronesis—the practical wisdom required to navigate complex, value-laden contexts—by augmenting human reasoning and decision-making within specific normative frameworks or take over social patterns (Agar, 2019). Furthermore, digital technologies are increasingly taking over social work through tools like communication platforms and robots designed for caregiving. A lively debate is unfolding about introducing large language models into therapeutic practice, including behavioral therapy (Stade et al., 2024). Communication platforms such as social media and messaging apps mediate how people connect, fostering relationships and enabling community building. At the same time, robots in elderly care, for example, assist with tasks ranging from companionship to physical support, addressing emotional and practical needs turning robots into a quasi-otherness (Ihde, 1990). These technologies do not just assist with social functions; they reshape the very nature of how we communicate, care, and connect, raising questions about how these changes impact human relationships and moral expectations.

2.2.4 The Malleability of Software

The normative and ethical challenges arising from the development and use of digital technologies are closely linked to their multi-purpose nature and dynamic adaptability. James H. Moor, in his influential essay, "What is Computer Ethics?" (Moor,

1985), describes the distinctive feature of digital technologies as "logically malleable." This characteristic enables their flexible application in previously unforeseeable contexts, leading to what he terms a "policy vacuum," a lack of normative orientation. In addition to the unpredictability of technological applications, Moor emphasizes that established ethical and legal categories must also be reconsidered. Hence, a defining feature of software is its *malleability of purpose*: it is often designed for one function but readily repurposed for another. A facial recognition model developed to unlock smartphones can just as easily be used for surveillance. This plasticity makes it difficult to anticipate all potential consequences at the design stage and calls for a heightened ethical sensitivity throughout a software system's lifecycle. In contrast to traditional tools whose use cases are relatively fixed, software systems continuously evolve through updates, user feedback, and recontextualization, which blurs the boundary between tool and application and between design and ethical responsibility.

At the same time, the multi-purpose nature of digital technologies underpins their economic strength. This surplus of potential applications creates what is known as *economies of scope*, the ability to quickly and easily repurpose technologies initially developed for a specific use for entirely different purposes. A classic early-twentieth-century example of economy of scope, aligning with the idea of repurposing technologies across different applications, is the automotive industry's expansion into military vehicle production during wartime. The core production techniques were originally optimized for civilian cars but were somewhat easily adapted for military purposes. Software extends this adaptation enormously. A striking example of far-reaching economy of scope in software is OpenAI's GPT models (or any other GenAI model for that matter), which have been repurposed across a diverse range of applications: from powering chatbots and generating code to enhancing educational tools, legal document analysis, and poetry.

While this flexibility makes digital technologies unique, it also complicates their alignment with specific fields of domain-specific ethics. The dynamic nature of digital technologies necessitates not only the development of regulatory frameworks but also the creation of practical, normative orientations that can be integrated into societal practices.

There is often no clear moral guidance or established practices for living ethically in a world shaped by digital technology. This lack of desirable habits and virtuous behavior stems from the rapid changes brought about by these technologies (Vallor, 2016). Simply following established moral rules, like "You shall not steal," does not guarantee the right actions in new contexts. For example, the theft of a digital file, such as an MP3, differs from stealing a physical CD, as the original owner retains access to the file even after it has been copied or distributed without permission, i.e., stolen. These rules are often tested by unfamiliar challenges, requiring us to rethink how they should be applied. In some cases, we may not fully understand the situation, which further complicates the issue, making it difficult to determine which moral principles are relevant.

2.2.5 The Imperceptible Nature of Software

One of the key features of software is its omnipresence, often combined with its imperceptibility (transparency in its original sense—meaning hard to perceive). Unlike traditional desktop computers, mobile devices such as smartphones and tablets—along with their interactions with other devices like cars or refrigerators—rely on middleware, sensors, and processes for seamless information exchange. This phenomenon, termed *ubiquitous computing*, includes adaptive, self-organizing systems that invisibly integrate into their environment.

Software's imperceptibility operates on two levels. First, we often do not see, hear, or feel its presence. Most software systems function so seamlessly precisely because they require no explicit input. Instead, our behavior serves as the input, sometimes without our awareness that we are being used as data points. Unlike physical technical objects, software exists in the hidden realm of cyberspace, quietly shaping and observing our interactions.

Second, software, particularly in the case of AI systems, can remain incomprehensible even when explicitly described. Its mechanisms are often so complex that they defy full understanding by both developers and users. This opaqueness underscores the ethical importance of explainability, ensuring users and decision-makers can understand the reasoning behind software's outcomes or at least take this opaqueness explicitly into account.

2.2.6 Persuasive Computing and the Ethical Challenge of Influence

This ethical significance is particularly apparent in persuasive computing, where software is designed to deliberately influence user behavior. By employing principles like trust and reciprocity, these systems can guide users toward desired actions, often without their explicit awareness. While this can lead to beneficial outcomes, such as promoting healthy habits, it raises concerns about intentional behavioral modification and the potential for manipulation.

In fields like ambient intelligence, the ethical stakes are even higher. In these systems, user input becomes less central as software analyzes behavioral data to predict and influence actions autonomously. These predictive algorithms often anticipate user preferences with such accuracy that they may surpass the users' own self-awareness—triggering Twitter founder and ex CEO Jack Dorsey to claim that the debate of social media is "no longer about freedom of speech, [but] about freedom of will" because "people have become so dependent on it [the algorithms], it's actually changing and impacting the agency we have" (Hetzner, 2024). This dynamic blurs the line between helpful guidance and intrusive control, demanding careful ethical scrutiny to ensure that these technologies respect user autonomy.

2.2.7 Social Power of Software

Digital artifacts are influential not only due to mass production and deployment but also their increasing use in social and emotional spheres, creating unprecedented power structures. They transform collective practices and open new realms of action, granting digital products and production practices immense power, most evident in platforms. These platforms such as Google, Amazon, and Facebook, initially designed for specific purposes, feature programmability, affordability, and data accessibility via APIs. Their modular software cores drive economic gains and user satisfaction but enforce proprietary standards, creating exclusivity and increasing opportunity costs due to network effects like larger user bases and richer exchanges. Over time, platforms have acquired infrastructure traits, such as ubiquity, reliability, and societal integration, influencing access to social and cultural goods.

While infrastructures aim for collective societal goals and are managed as public goods, platforms blur these lines, regulating interpersonal and economic interactions. They enable millions to communicate globally at minimal cost, offering new opportunities but also concentrating power. Platform operators gain access to vast user bases, influence behaviors, and control information flows, raising ethical concerns about exclusion and participation in vital social practices, as highlighted in debates on Internet access as a human right. On the other hand, software has the potential to empower individuals by reducing information asymmetries and shifting power dynamics in various domains. For instance, the Internet has historically leveled the playing field between buyers and sellers by providing consumers with greater access to product information, reviews, and price comparisons. This transparency has often pressured sellers to adopt more honest and customer-centric practices. Similarly, digital platforms and algorithmic tools can enhance user autonomy, enabling individuals to make more informed decisions, advocate for their interests, and hold institutions accountable. We need to acknowledge this aspect of software when we develop and deploy it—realizing that it usually cuts both ways.

2.2.8 Diffusion of Responsibility

Even though responsibility diffusion is a familiar phenomenon, Helen Nissenbaum highlights why it might be even more pronounced in the software industry. Regardless of the organizational structure, developer culture, as Helen Nissenbaum (1994) argues, tends to dismiss normative issues too quickly. She identifies four prevalent attitudes systematically embedded in the work culture of software development: the many-hands problem, the bug culture, ownership, and the scapegoat trap.

The many-hands problem refers to the difficulty that arises when many people are involved in software development, making it challenging to attribute decisions or errors to a single individual. The varying competencies of entrepreneurs, managers, and technical staff, including graphic designers, quality assurance experts, security professionals, and users, lead to a diffusion of responsibility. Such diffusion not only complicates the attribution of responsibility ex post but also fosters, ex ante, an attitude of responsibility delegation or indifference.

The term bug culture describes a culture of indifference toward software errors. The occurrence of faulty software is seen as inevitable because software can never be perfect (this is related to the discussion in "The Relative Triviality of Manufacturing and Distribution" above). Framing errors as "just bugs" deflects potential moral significance. According to Nissenbaum, this leads to a culture of disregarding quality assurance, including normative concerns. This indifferent attitude is further reinforced by the complexity of the systems, as verifying software cannot be achieved by an individual alone, potentially resulting in moral overload. Consequently, undesirable results can neither technically nor organizationally be attributed to a specific decision or action. Decision-makers in this context include policymakers, companies, developers, and users.

At the corporate level, there is often little mandatory assumption or ownership of responsibility: Once the code ships, creators often feel their responsibility ends, and any misuse or downstream impact is now the owner's or user's problem. This is a consequence of the popular instrumental view of technology, which we discussed above.

The computer (and the software running on it) increasingly serves as a scapegoat: the computer is blamed, not the entrepreneur, the developer, or the user. Errors and undesirable results, whether in the form of output or outcomes, are attributed to the software itself, as it shapes contexts of perception and action structures. If this is not possible, then organizations may single out a convenient individual (or small group) for blame, masking the deeper, systemic causes embedded in the structure of the development process or organizational culture.

This unique responsibility issue in information technology and engineering demands a model of technical traceability and documentation, as well as processes that enable an organizational design of responsibility attribution defined by areas of competence. This requires employees who perceive themselves as autonomous, enabling them to become aware of their decision-making power.

References

Agar, N. (2019). *How to be human in the digital economy*. MIT Press.
Aristotle. (350 B.C./2014). In R. Crisp (Ed.) *Nicomachean ethics* (2nd ed.). Cambridge University Press.
Heidegger, M. (1977). *The question concerning technology, and other essays*. Harper & Row.
Hetzner, C. (2024, June 6). Twitter founder Jack Dorsey warns social media algorithms are draining people of their free will—And Elon Musk agrees with him. *Fortune*. Retrieved from https://fortune.com/2024/06/06/elon-musk-jack-dorsey-twitter-x-social-media-algorithms-free-will
Ihde, D. (1990). *Technology and the lifeworld: From garden to earth*. Indiana University Press.

References

Moor, J. H. (1985). What is computer ethics. *Metaphilosophy, 16*(4), 266–275.
Nida-Rümelin, J. (2023). *A theory of practical reason*. Palgrave Macmillan.
Nissenbaum, H. (1994). Computing and accountability. *Communications of the ACM, 37*(1), 72–81.
Nyholm, S. (2022). *This is technology ethics: An introduction*. John Wiley & Sons.
Recki, B. (2021). Technik als Form der Freiheit. Kant über Handlungsrationalität in Kultur und Natur. In B. Himmelmann & C. Serck-Hanssen (Eds.), *The court of reason: Proceedings of the 13th International Kant Congress*. Walter de Gruyter.
Stade, E. C., Stirman, S. W., Ungar, L. H., Boland, C. L., Schwartz, H. A., Yaden, D. B., et al. (2024). Large language models could change the future of behavioral healthcare: A proposal for responsible development and evaluation. *NPJ Mental Health Research, 3*(1), 12.
Susser, D., Roessler, B., & Nissenbaum, H. (2019). Technology, autonomy, and manipulation. *Internet policy review, 8*(2), 1–22.
Vallor, S. (2016). *Technology and the virtues: A philosophical guide to a future worth wanting*. Oxford University Press.

Open Access This chapter is licensed under the terms of the Creative Commons Attribution 4.0 International License (http://creativecommons.org/licenses/by/4.0/), which permits use, sharing, adaptation, distribution and reproduction in any medium or format, as long as you give appropriate credit to the original author(s) and the source, provide a link to the Creative Commons license and indicate if changes were made.

The images or other third party material in this chapter are included in the chapter's Creative Commons license, unless indicated otherwise in a credit line to the material. If material is not included in the chapter's Creative Commons license and your intended use is not permitted by statutory regulation or exceeds the permitted use, you will need to obtain permission directly from the copyright holder.

Chapter 3
Why Develop Software Ethically?

> "It is not living that should be our priority, but living well."
> Socrates in Plato's Crito (399 B.C.E./2024)

Abstract This chapter explores the ethical imperative for software development, emphasizing the inherent embedding of values in technology and its profound impact on individual behavior and societal norms. Unlike traditional tools, software actively mediates user experiences and often operates beyond users' awareness, shaping decisions and interactions through algorithms and interfaces. Recognizing this, the chapter argues for an anticipatory and proactive ethical stance, integrating ethical considerations from the outset of the development process through deployment and maintenance. The uniqueness of software systems presents unique ethical challenges, notably the distribution and diffusion of responsibility. Responsibility cannot be adequately addressed by mere legal compliance or industry standards. Instead, it must encompass organizational culture, interdisciplinary collaboration, and ongoing ethical reflection throughout the software lifecycle. Practical approaches discussed include embedding ethical reflection into development processes, engaging diverse stakeholders, and fostering a shared sense of responsibility across development teams and organizational hierarchies. The chapter also critically assesses principle-based and bottom-up ethical frameworks, advocating for a dynamic hybrid approach that combines universal ethical principles with context-sensitive, participatory methods. This discursive approach emphasizes collaborative ethical deliberation, empowering developers, managers, and organizations to anticipate and address ethical concerns proactively.

In the previous chapter, we saw that digital technology is not always a neutral tool but a mediator of human perception, action, and social norms. This raises a central ethical question: if technology transforms our experience of the world, who is responsible for these transformations? In today's digitally driven society, software shapes the world we inhabit, influencing individual choices, interactions, and broader societal dynamics. Yet despite its significant impact, ethical considerations in software development often remain an afterthought, overshadowed by technical and commercial priorities. This chapter aims to address this gap by exploring why ethical considerations are not just beneficial but essential in software creation. By examining how values become embedded within technological artifacts and how these shape user experiences and social structures, we will uncover why software development must proactively integrate ethics from the earliest stages of design and throughout the entire development lifecycle. In other words: The uniqueness and potential impact of software systems bring us in a state of normative urgency—thus creating the necessity that ethical deliberation must be involved early.

If we accept the claim that values are inherently embedded in software, shaping both the world through its impact on users, and that unlike traditional tools, software often limits the control users have over its functions and effects, we realize that in many cases, users may not even be aware that their actions are being guided or influenced by underlying algorithms. This lack of transparency can profoundly impact decision-making, for instance, when behavioral data is used to nudge users in particular directions. Moreover, shifting the normative foundations of social subsystems through software can fundamentally alter how we engage within basic social structures, such as education or work environments. For instance, digital learning platforms or the use of large language models as tutors can redefine the dynamics of student-teacher interactions, while workplace communication tools can reshape organizational culture and power dynamics. This capacity to transform the norms of entire social systems underscores the ethical responsibility of developers to consider the broader impacts of their technologies.

When we talk about the ethical responsibility of technology producers, it is not enough to focus solely on legal compliance or meeting industry standards. If companies truly wish to see themselves as moral actors, their responsibility must extend beyond mere rule-following. This means actively shaping the conditions for ethical development and embedding these values into the organizational culture (Chap. 8). However, this raises important questions: How should responsibility be understood in this context? Who exactly is responsible, and why is it important to involve different perspectives from the very beginning of the development process by—for instance— including relevant stakeholders? Responsibility in this context is not just about the actions of individual developers or project managers. It also includes the broader organizational structures that guide technological innovation. This means distributing responsibility across teams, empowering them to make ethically informed decisions at every stage of the development process. But why should responsibility be shared so broadly, and why should it be integrated from the outset? Simply put, the ethical impacts of technology are rarely the result of a single decision or oversight. Instead, they emerge from a complex network of choices, trade-offs, and interactions, making it essential to involve all relevant actors from the beginning.

In this chapter, we will explore how the inherent embedding of values in technology leads to the need to take an anticipatory ethical stance. This means that ethical considerations must be integrated into the design and development of technology from the very beginning. We will argue that companies must see themselves as moral actors if they are to fully grasp the ethical responsibilities of their software engineering teams.

After outlining why it is essential to take moral responsibility from the outset and maintain it throughout the entire lifecycle of a technology, we will discuss practical approaches to ethical design. Finally, we will consider whether these approaches should be primarily principle based, emphasizing universal ethical standards, or bottom-up, focusing on the lived experiences and practical insights of those involved in the development process.

3.1 Why Anticipatory or Proactive Ethics?

As Chap. 2 explained, digital technologies may be value-laden artefacts whose inner workings lie far beyond the user's immediate control—what sets it apart from a simple tool such as a hammer. Because of this built-in mediation, the ethical burden moves upstream: moral responsibility now rests also with the producers and ultimately with the development team that shapes what the technology will do. This is called an anticipatory stance toward technology ethics (Brey, 2012), which includes that ethical challenges and ethical desirable aspects need to be taken into account already while designing, developing, and even deploying software systems—in short, throughout the lifecycle of a product. Ethical engineering is thus more than accompanying ethical research or technology assessment. It is the endeavor to design and develop software systems that align with our values and that foster desirable values right from the beginning (Zuber et al., 2024).

Technology assessment (TA) now sits at the heart of innovation policy, yet by itself, it falls short of the ethical scrutiny today's digital systems require. As a systematic, interdisciplinary exercise, technology assessment tries to anticipate and analyze the social, economic, environmental, and ethical consequences of emerging or existing technologies. Its goal is to inform policymakers, industry, and the public by mapping potential risks, benefits, and trade-offs—often through scenario studies and stakeholder consultation—so that decisions about research, regulation, and deployment can be made responsibly. We argue that technology assessment alone is not sufficient for addressing the ethical challenges of modern technology. While TA is effective at identifying potential risks and benefits, it typically focuses on outcomes rather than the processes that shape a technology's design and implementation. This approach often overlooks the values embedded in technical systems, which can influence user behavior, reinforce power dynamics, and reshape social norms in ways that are not immediately visible. Moreover, TA is usually retrospective, responding to issues as they arise rather than anticipating them from the start. To ensure that technology aligns with broader societal values, a more comprehensive approach is needed: one that integrates ethical reflection throughout the entire lifecycle of a technology, from design to deployment and beyond.

Due to the unique nature of software products, they cannot be evaluated or "approved" as easily as traditional industrial goods. As a result, the focus should shift from solely assessing the final product to also considering the development process and the training of the teams involved. In this context, concepts like a "Software TÜV" or some other safety organization that merely certify a finished model might overlook critical aspects of ethical software design. Instead, ongoing oversight, continuous improvement, and the cultivation of ethical awareness throughout the software lifecycle become essential to ensuring responsible technology. This question clearly touches on the challenge of accountability in the context of complex software systems. It reflects the "many hands problem," where responsibility for outcomes is dispersed across numerous actors, stages, and components, making it difficult to pinpoint accountability.

In the case of software development, this complexity arises from the fact that systems are not created in isolation. Instead, they are built using a wide array of pre-existing libraries, third-party components, and interconnected platforms. The responsibility for unintended outcomes or ethical breaches often becomes blurred as a result. Developers rely on software libraries, integrate third-party APIs, and depend on open-source contributions, all of which complicate the task of identifying who is responsible for potential failures or harms.

Moreover, software systems often evolve over time, with multiple developers contributing at different stages of their lifecycle. This means that pinpointing a single moment or decision as the "critical point of responsibility" is rarely straightforward. The challenge is not only technical but also deeply ethical, as it requires tracing accountability through a web of interactions, dependencies, and decisions.

Therefore, finding effective ways to assign responsibility in this context demands both technical solutions, like better documentation and transparency, and ethical frameworks that can accommodate the distributed nature of software development. This might involve rethinking conventional approaches to accountability and adopting more robust mechanisms for tracing decision-making across the entire software lifecycle.

In their essay *Responsible Technology Design: Conversations for Success*, Winter and Butler (2021) identify a fundamental paradox in how responsibility is assigned in technology development. Software engineers are often viewed as solely accountable for both the positive and negative impacts of digital technologies. This perspective overlooks a critical aspect: not all ethical challenges can be addressed through technical solutions alone. A normatively desirable design approach should not merely aim to prevent harm but also proactively promote positive values and behaviors. This anticipatory stance is characterized by a commitment to ethical principles, such as inclusivity and transparency, which can be operationalized, for example, through accessible design and meaningful user consent mechanisms. Responsibility, in this sense, extends beyond avoiding harm to actively affirming and embedding values worth pursuing throughout the technology lifecycle.

Winter and Butler emphasize that expecting software engineers to independently identify and address every normative concern is unrealistic and even counterproductive, as it would demand superhuman capabilities. This highlights the importance of shared responsibility, requiring collaboration across disciplines and organizational levels to fully address the complex ethical landscape of digital technologies.

The concept of moral overload has been extensively discussed in other fields, such as healthcare, where professionals often face internal moral conflict (Gräb-Schmidt, 2018). In these contexts, caregivers may struggle either because they fail to recognize an ethical imbalance (an epistemic shortfall, which we will explore in Chaps. 6 and 7) or because they feel pressured to act against their own moral convictions (Chap. 8). Both moral uncertainty and moral pressure not only impede ethical reflection but also make it more difficult to articulate one's moral stance. Nevertheless, this does not imply that responsibility cannot be assigned to companies and development teams.

3.2 The Moral Responsibility of Software Production Companies

Ethical considerations in software development are not merely ancillary or optional. They are integral to the responsibilities of developers, engineers, and organizations as moral agents. Every development decision shapes the behavior of technological systems and, by extension, the lives of individuals and societies they affect. To act as a moral agent is to acknowledge this influence and to take responsibility for the consequences that emerge from one's actions. This responsibility does not come without costs; engaging in ethically informed development processes requires investments of time, financial resources, and expertise. The extent of these investments varies depending on the context and potential risk associated with the product or system being developed. Individual software engineers rarely possess the authority to steer the overall direction of a product. They typically operate within larger organizational structures that define the strategic objectives, allocate resources, and assign roles according to hierarchical decision rights. In practice, an engineer's decision space is often confined to a narrow segment of the development process—writing code, implementing features, or optimizing system components—while the broader questions of what should be built, for whom, and to what end are resolved elsewhere, often at the level of product leadership or executive management. As a result, the ethically foundational question—Should this product be developed at all?—belongs primarily to the domain of business ethics and corporate responsibility. In contrast, the question that individual engineers and development teams are more realistically positioned to answer is: Given that we are to develop this product, how can we do so in a normatively desirable way? Of course, in extreme cases—such as when a project clearly violates laws or fundamental moral norms—one may reasonably expect an engineer to refuse participation. Yet in most real-world scenarios, where ethical trade-offs are ambiguous and employment is at stake, such acts of refusal are both rare and costly. This underscores the importance of embedding ethical responsibility at the organizational level, not merely relying on the conscience or resistance of individual developers. We will talk about organizational factors in the last chapter. Yet it is important to understand that software is a unique form of technology—as we have mentioned earlier. In some cases—particularly in Web-based platforms and applications—it is common for individual engineers or small teams to independently code and deploy features. This level of autonomy is often celebrated as a core aspect of the company's engineering culture. Even in organizations with more conventional development processes, certain updates—such as bug fixes—are regularly released with only technical oversight (Vallor & Narayanan, 2021).

In any case, the question remains: why should companies be willing to bear these costs and consider ethical issues or even spend the resources to let developers design and code software systems ethically?

There are several compelling reasons. First, the risk of legal and reputational damage cannot be underestimated. While legal consequences require formal violations of laws or regulations, reputational harm often arises from the public's perception that a company has failed to act in accordance with prevailing social norms. This kind of damage may occur even in the absence of formal wrongdoing and can have lasting consequences for a company's brand, investor relations, and consumer trust. These risks have grown even more salient in light of recent regulatory developments, particularly the European Union's Artificial Intelligence Act (EU AI Act). The Act introduces a comprehensive risk-based framework for AI systems, distinguishing between unacceptable, high-risk, limited-risk, and minimal-risk applications. High-risk systems, such as those deployed in education, employment, law enforcement, or critical infrastructure, are subject to rigorous requirements. These include data governance obligations, transparency and human oversight mechanisms, and robust risk management procedures. Compliance is enforced through ex ante conformity assessments, third-party audits, and mandatory technical documentation. Fines for violations can reach €35 million or 7% of global annual turnover. While the AI Act provides a legal structure that organizations must adhere to, it is important to recognize that ethics goes beyond compliance. Laws define minimum standards for acceptable behavior; ethical responsibility requires striving for what is *right*, not just what is *permissible*.

In parallel to legal obligations, companies also face increasing pressure from society. As Bénabou and Tirole (2010) have noted, ethical responsibility is very likely a normal good, which means that as societies become more affluent, demand for ethical behavior increases. In this environment, the public expects more than technical competence or regulatory adherence; it expects proactive engagement with moral questions. Companies that fail to meet these expectations risk becoming targets of public criticism and losing their social license to operate. Ethical engagement, therefore, is not just a matter of legal foresight but of social legitimacy.

Moreover, ethical motivation is not limited to external demands. Many organizations and software professionals are intrinsically motivated to create systems that reflect their personal values and moral convictions—just because it is *the right thing to do*. As Adam Smith eloquently observed, "Man naturally desires, not only to be loved, but to be lovely; or to be that thing which is the natural and proper object of love" (Smith, 1759). This longing to be morally admirable is a powerful force. Development teams do not operate in moral isolation; they are embedded in social and professional structures where ethical expectations are ever present. Organizations that recognize and support this intrinsic motivation can cultivate stronger internal cultures of responsibility and trust.

This internal moral climate is further reinforced by changing dynamics in the labor market. In the IT sector, there is a pronounced shortage of skilled professionals, resulting in a seller's market for talent. Under these conditions, developers increasingly prioritize working for companies that align with their ethical values. The Cone Communications Millennial Employee Study (Cone, 2016) found that 64% of young professionals would not accept a job at a company lacking a corporate social responsibility (CSR) strategy, and 83% stated that their loyalty increases when employers engage seriously with ethical and social issues. Wespire (2020) similarly reported that millennials are the first generation to prioritize purpose over salary. Companies like Microsoft have already begun responding to this shift through initiatives such as "People Empowerment," which aim to foster value-driven and ethically engaged work environments.

3.3 The Responsibility of Software Creators

Once technology is understood not as a neutral tool but as a mediator of human experience that influences and shapes human experiences, perceptions, and interactions, the normative burden shifts from the moment of use to the moment of design. Those who define, implement, prioritize, and deploy software are not merely solving technical problems. They are actively influencing the world their users inhabit. This constitutes the ethical responsibility of the production side. The ACM Code opens with the unambiguous reminder that "Computing professionals' actions change the world" (Gotterbarn et al., 2018): by writing requirements, selecting data, choosing an architecture, or accepting a user-story as *done*, production-side actors bring a particular sociotechnical reality into being. Here, we want to provide a very brief discussion of responsibility that we will pick up during the course of the book. Even in its brevity, this discussion is intended to offer a lens through which the subsequent chapters may be better understood. We will refer to the relevant chapters.

The main goal to foster ethical software development is to distribute obligations and responsibilities across the various functions of a software organization (Chap. 8 will try to shed some light on it). However, before we can do this, we must first establish what it means to be responsible for a sociotechnical artefact. Now more than ever, it is essential to reaffirm that responsibility applies solely to *moral agents*, and within this category degrees of accountability may differ. The only entities we can confidently regard as moral agents are human beings. Artificial-intelligence systems—whatever their future potential—do not meet the criteria for moral agency; consequently, they cannot legitimately be singled out for praise or blame. We attribute responsibility not only to single persons but also, by extension, to collectives such as groups and organizations. Yet when we hold an organization to account, we tacitly acknowledge that it is the individual people within it who ultimately bear that responsibility.

The classical debate in moral philosophy typically reduces responsibility to two jointly necessary conditions: The first condition is called the *epistemic (or knowledge)* condition, which requires that an agent must have been aware, or able to be aware, of what they were doing and of the likely consequences and moral significance of the act. The ACM Code states, for instance, that software professionals shall "perform work only in areas of competence" and to "maintain high standards of professional competence, conduct, and ethical practice" (ibid.). This means that the responsibility of the producer is to ensure that a high level of knowledge regarding the technology and its impacts must be constantly maintained and fostered as technology and knowledge about the impact of technology progresses. Principle 2.5. makes this very clear: "Give comprehensive and thorough evaluations of computer systems and their impacts, including analysis of possible risks." In Chap. 6, we will discuss the issues of "spotting the right," that is, how to create the necessary knowledge to enable ethically informed software development.

Second is control (or freedom), which states that the agent must have had sufficient volitional control, i.e., the ability to do otherwise. They need to possess the decision-making authority (practical ability to alter the product). Above we cited the ACM code claiming that "computing professionals' actions change the world." At first glance, this may sound grandiose, full of pathos, or even bordering on arrogance. After all, every action, in some minimal sense, changes the world (ever so little). Yet there is truth to the claim: the decisions made by computing professionals often have far-reaching consequences. It is therefore essential to recognize the limits of individual control in software development. Earlier, we discussed the "many hands problem" and how responsibility becomes diffused across teams, leading to an implicit loss of individual agency. Beyond that, we must also consider the organizational context in which most software is produced. Software development typically occurs within structured institutions, where control and freedom to act are necessarily constrained to maintain coordination and efficiency. Decision-making authority is rarely distributed evenly; instead, it tends to follow hierarchical patterns. Advocates of agile methodologies might object, but even in agile environments, hierarchies persist, if only in the form of strategic decisions about what to build, which often rests with upper management. Chapter 8 will deal with this particular issue. This problem is not unique to software. In aviation, the safety of a commercial aircraft depends on thousands of decisions made by designers, engineers, pilots, and regulators—yet no single individual is wholly responsible for its safety or failure. In civil engineering, licensed professionals are legally accountable for safety-critical decisions, providing a clear point of ethical and legal responsibility. By contrast, in software development, such accountability structures are often underdeveloped. The software industry can learn from these mature fields by creating layers of responsibility, including formal review processes, clearly assigned ethical ownership, and escalation mechanisms.

In the literature of engineering ethics, a third element is often additionally mentioned: causal contribution. Strictly speaking, causal participation is presupposed in the two conditions (one can, for instance, hardly control an outcome to which one makes no relevant causal difference), yet making that premise explicit may help trace responsibility through distributed and large teams.

Within software development, responsibility is divided. On one axis lies the *technological artefact itself*: the data structures, the algorithmic architecture, the control flow hidden in a pull-request, etc. Here, moral agency attaches most directly to those who create and modify code: individual coders, review teams, UX designers, and product owners. They possess the granular control over causal mechanisms, the situated knowledge of design choices, and the professional foresight to anticipate technical failure modes. On the other axis lies the *domain of application*: the business model that decides where and why the software will intervene in social life. Should a recommender optimize for user engagement or for civic discourse? Should a short-term-rental platform scale until urban housing supply is distorted? These questions sit squarely with senior product leadership and the C-suite, because only they command the strategic levers that set incentives, allocate resources, and choose markets. When Airbnb listings eclipse affordable rental stock, or ride-sharing fleets overwhelm public transit, the ethical deficit is not a coding error: it is a governance and a political decision.

This illustrates that software development teams consist of a wide range of roles, each contributing to the overall design, functionality, and impact of the final product (Table 3.1). At the core are developers and coders, who write and modify code, implement algorithms, and manage data structures. They hold significant ethical responsibility, as their technical choices directly shape how the software behaves and interacts with users. Code review teams add a critical layer of oversight, ensuring that code is of high quality, consistent, and free from harmful bugs or biases. UX/UI designers influence user behavior and decision-making through the design of interfaces, potentially embedding ethical concerns like privacy, consent, and accessibility into the user experience.

At a higher level, product owners and managers bridge the gap between technical teams and business goals, prioritizing features and aligning project scope with user needs. This group is crucial for balancing market demands with ethical

Table 3.1 Roles and responsibilities in ethical software development

Role	Responsibilities	Ethical considerations
Developers and coders	Writing and modifying code, implementing algorithms	Technical failures, security vulnerabilities, fairness in decision-making
Code Review teams	Reviewing code quality and consistency	Preventing harmful code decisions, ensuring transparency
UX/UI designers	Designing user interfaces and experiences	Shaping user behavior, avoiding dark patterns
Product owners and managers	Defining project scope, prioritizing features	Balancing market demands with ethical design
Senior product leadership and C-suite	Setting strategic direction, resource allocation	Impact on public good vs. commercial gain
Data scientists and ML engineers	Developing models, managing data pipelines	Addressing bias, fairness, and privacy issues
Compliance officers and legal teams	Ensuring legal and regulatory compliance	Preventing unethical practices, reducing legal risk
Ethicists and ethics committees	Providing ethical oversight, developing guidelines	Aligning technology with values

considerations, ensuring that profit motives do not compromise user autonomy or well-being. Senior product leadership and C-suite executives set the strategic direction for the company, making decisions about target markets, resource allocation, and business models. These choices often have profound ethical implications, as they determine the broader social impact of the technology.

Additionally, data scientists and machine learning engineers play a critical role, using data to refine algorithms and improve model accuracy while also bearing responsibility for addressing issues like bias and fairness. Compliance officers and legal teams provide a final layer of accountability, ensuring that software adheres to legal and ethical standards, while ethicists and ethics committees guide the overall ethical direction of the company, helping align technology with broader societal values.

3.4 Approaches to Ethical Software Development

As we demonstrated, ethical responsibility in software development is not merely a cost to be minimized but a strategic and moral imperative. And yet significant challenges remain. There is no universal certificate for being an ethical software engineer. No consensus exists on what exactly constitutes a good software engineer in ethical terms. Values vary across cultural, industrial, and organizational contexts, and the applications of technology span public and private sectors alike. Hence, unlike in fields such as medicine, there is no unified professional goal or clearly defined societal domain that provides a shared value framework to which all software development teams or companies are uniformly accountable.

Despite this complexity, several conceptual approaches have emerged to help structure ethical engagement. Hagendorff (2022) distinguishes between three approaches: *ethics by design*, which embeds moral reasoning directly into AI systems; *ethics in design*, which structures development processes to support ethical outcomes; and *ethics for design*, which emphasizes the moral integrity and reflection of the designers themselves. These approaches are not mutually exclusive; rather, they represent different entry points for addressing the multifaceted ethical challenges of software development.

3.4.1 Principle-Based and Bottom-Up Approaches

Approaches to ethical decision-making in software engineering tend to swing between two poles. At one extreme lie principle-based, top-down frameworks that deduce what *ought* to be done from universal values; at the other are bottom-up, context-sensitive practices that arise from the lived realities of coding, deployment, and maintenance. With that in mind, the following discussion turns first to the limits of relying solely on a principle-based approach. A principle-based approach

3.4 Approaches to Ethical Software Development

typically relies on abstract, universal norms such as fairness, autonomy, or transparency and seeks to guide action by deducing what is ethically permissible or desirable from these predefined values. For example, the principle of *non-maleficence* (do no harm), drawn from applied ethics, might guide developers to avoid releasing software that could cause harm to users. Likewise, organizational tools such as Codes of Conduct (CoCs) aim to formalize such principles within a professional context, offering developers a reference for expected behavior. However, these principles are often too vague or rigid to offer concrete guidance in the face of the complex, ambiguous, and rapidly evolving conditions that characterize software development. They must be translated into context-specific actions, a process that is neither straightforward nor free of interpretation. Furthermore, real-world ethical challenges often resist reduction to any single overarching principle, and the pace of technological change can lead to ethical blind spots or delayed responses.

Complementing this is the bottom-up approach, which emphasizes situated ethical deliberation, moral intuition, and the cultivation of ethical sensitivity within concrete development contexts. Rather than starting with abstract norms, bottom-up methods begin with real-world experiences, stakeholder perspectives, and team-based reflection to guide ethical decision-making. An illustrative method here is Value Sensitive Design (VSD), which integrates stakeholder input throughout the design and development lifecycle to ensure that software aligns with human values. Another example is the use of stakeholder workshops or participatory design sessions where users, developers, and affected parties collaboratively explore ethical concerns and co-develop value-aligned solutions. While more adaptive and responsive, such methods may lack formal consistency and can struggle with scalability or normative justification. In the absence of a shared evaluative framework, ethical judgments may become fragmented, overly subjective, or susceptible to the influence of dominant voices within a team or organization.

Therefore, rather than relying exclusively on either abstract normative principles or unstructured contextual judgments, we must strive for a dynamic ethical architecture: one that integrates normative ethical theories (such as deontology, virtue ethics, or care ethics), participatory and iterative design methods like VSD, and the cultivation of professional virtues such as integrity, responsibility, and humility. This hybrid model allows for moral reasoning that is both principled and responsive, combining normative depth with practical sensitivity. It is better equipped to accommodate the complexities of modern software development, where ethical responsibility is neither static nor singular but emergent, distributed, and deeply embedded within sociotechnical systems.

To genuinely take responsibility seriously, organizations must adopt approaches that combine principle-based ethics with bottom-up, practice-oriented strategies. Principle-based approaches provide a clear normative framework, offering guidance on what is considered right or wrong. However, these must be complemented by bottom-up approaches that capture the lived experiences and practical wisdom of those directly involved in the development process. This combination ensures that ethical considerations are not just abstract guidelines but are deeply integrated into everyday decision-making.

3.4.2 Why a Discursive Ethical Approach?

A proactive ethical stance in technology development necessitates collaborative mediation, specifically, a jointly conducted discursive process that identifies normatively relevant facts during the development phase itself (Nida-Rümelin, 1999). In this context, ethical evaluation is not treated as an external or retrospective consideration but is embedded from the outset alongside questions of technical feasibility. This approach reflects a participatory ethos, emphasizing shared responsibility and early, inclusive engagement with ethical questions.

Such a process serves not only to identify ethically significant aspects of a given technology but also to support collective decision-making on which ethical concerns are imperative to pursue and how these should be translated into concrete technical responses. By doing so, it fosters a co-creative design culture in which ethical reflection is embedded as a living practice within the routines of development work.

Within this stance, ethical anticipation is understood not as a solitary expert activity but as a discursive process: a collaborative effort to deliberate on facts, values, and potential futures. This structure helps reduce moral distress, as it supports moral responsibility through cultivated attitudes of "identifying" and "speaking for oneself." These are enacted through participatory routines that empower individuals to recognize ethical tensions and express their moral perspectives. Drawing on the principles of discursive ethics (Chap. 6), this approach situates moral legitimacy in inclusive, reasoned dialogue among all those affected. The aim is not merely to anticipate outcomes but to democratize the design process by incorporating diverse voices into value articulation and ethical foresight.

Since the 1970s, however, the dominance of empirical technology assessment focused primarily on economic and sociological evaluations for policymaking (van den Burg & Swierstra, 2013), which has contributed to a decline in normative discourse within technology ethics. Shannon Vallor (2016) has described this development as the "empirical turn," which led to a proliferation of isolated case studies often devoid of a shared theoretical framework, resulting in a fragmented landscape of ethical insights. Despite this fragmentation, Vallor (2016) argues that empirical analysis remains valuable, as it can "feed" practical reason and thus enrich the very deliberative processes that discursive ethics depend on (Chap. 6).

Against this backdrop, a procedural and participatory ethics must also be anticipatory. It involves the integration of forward-looking ethical reflection into the design process in order to ensure continuous normative evaluation (Brey, 2012; Palm & Hansson, 2006; Stahl et al., 2016; Wright, 2011). Brey (2012) distinguishes two modes of anticipatory ethics: speculative and conservative. The speculative mode uses structured foresight methods, such as the Delphi technique (Häder & Häder, 2000), to generate and assess a range of potential future scenarios based on their ethical desirability. In contrast, the conservative mode focuses on intended uses and foreseeable outcomes, deliberately limiting its scope to avoid speculation about indeterminate external applications.

In sum, what is needed is an anticipatory ethics that is embedded into development processes and carried out by trained, ethically reflective managers and developers (Chap. 8). They must be capable of identifying ethically relevant issues, making justified decisions, implementing them in design, and evaluating their impact. However, this responsibility cannot rest on individuals alone, especially not under conditions of pressure or isolation. Instead, it requires collaborative, discursive practices, ideally focused on the intended deployment and use of the software system.

Against this backdrop, we turn to the question of how such identification and deliberation processes can be conducted systematically, without falling into the trap of value arbitrariness. This requires a principled yet participatory approach, one that combines normative ethical theories with bottom-up engagement.

3.5 Conclusion

In this chapter, we have argued that the ethical responsibility of software developers and technology companies extends far beyond mere compliance or retrospective assessment. Given the inherent value-laden nature of digital technology and the often-diminished control users have over their interactions with software, it is clear that responsibility must be proactively integrated throughout the entire lifecycle of a product. This anticipatory stance emphasizes the importance of embedding ethical reflection at every stage of design, development, and deployment, rather than treating ethics as an afterthought.

Technology assessment (TA) alone is insufficient for this task. While TA can effectively identify potential risks and benefits, it tends to focus on outcomes rather than the processes that shape a technology's design and use. It often overlooks the deeply embedded values that shape user behavior, reinforce social norms, and influence power dynamics. These values are not mere technical features but constitute a fundamental part of the technology itself, making it essential to consider ethical implications from the outset.

Moreover, the unique nature of software means that simple certification or "approval" approaches, like a hypothetical "Software TÜV," are not enough to ensure ethical outcomes. Instead, ongoing oversight, continuous improvement, and the cultivation of ethical awareness are necessary to address the full spectrum of ethical challenges. This approach acknowledges that software systems are not static artifacts but evolving sociotechnical constructs that continually shape and are shaped by the societies they serve.

Finally, we highlighted the need for shared responsibility within development teams and across organizational levels. Expecting individual software engineers to independently resolve all ethical challenges is neither realistic nor fair. Responsibility must be distributed, involving not only developers but also designers, product managers, data scientists, compliance officers, and executives. Only through collaborative, interdisciplinary engagement can we hope to address the complex, often unforeseen ethical challenges that arise in software development.

The idea of aligning software systems with moral values resonates strongly with the principles of Human-Computer Interaction (HCI) design, which emphasizes creating technologies that are not just functional but also ethically sound and human centered. In HCI, the concept of embedded values is particularly relevant, as it acknowledges that the design choices embedded in digital artifacts can reflect and reinforce specific values. For instance, designing a software system that prioritizes user autonomy, privacy, and transparency aligns well with the established HCI principles of usability and user empowerment. Just as the software/computer ethics field has converged on a core set of values, HCI also seeks to ensure that technologies promote desirable human experiences, mitigate harm, and respect the diverse needs of users. Moreover, the role of regulators and governments in setting these standards underscores the importance of aligning both technical and ethical considerations in design, ensuring that digital systems contribute positively to society.

As we move forward, the challenge will be to apply methods that combine principle-based ethics with bottom-up, context-sensitive approaches, ensuring that ethical considerations are not just abstract guidelines but deeply integrated into everyday decision-making. This hybrid approach will be essential for creating technology that not only minimizes harm but actively promotes human flourishing and social good.

Therefore, what is needed is a technologically informed, ethically aware professional who understands where to focus their attention in order to reduce moral distress and uncertainty. Such a professional must recognize that it is not only possible but also necessary to act ethically within the technical and organizational constraints of their role. This requires a clear understanding of the ethical dimensions of technology design, an awareness of the impact of their decisions, and the confidence to make morally informed choices in complex, real-world contexts.

With this foundation in place, we will now turn our attention to what can be learned from ethics as a discipline, exploring how its principles and methods can be effectively integrated into the practice of software development.

References

Bénabou, R., & Tirole, J. (2010). Individual and corporate social responsibility. *Economica, 77*(305), 1–19.

Brey, P. A. (2012). Anticipating ethical issues in emerging IT. *Ethics and Information Technology, 14*(4), 305–317.

Cone. (2016). *Cone communications millennial employee engagement study*. Retrieved from https://calisanbagliligi.wordpress.com/wp-content/uploads/2019/10/75bb1-2016conecommunicationsmillennialemployeeengagementstudy_pressreleaseandfactsheet.pdf

Gotterbarn, D. W., Brinkman, B., Flick, C., Kirkpatrick, M. S., Miller, K., Vazansky, K. et al. (2018). ACM code of ethics and professional conduct. Association for Computing Machinery.

References

Gräb-Schmidt, E. & Stritzelberger, C. P. (2018). Ethische Herausforderungen durch autonome Systeme und Robotik im Bereich der Pflege. *Zeitschrift für medizinische Ethik, 64*(4), 357–372.

Häder, M., & Häder, S. (Eds.). (2000). *Die Delphi-Technik in den Sozialwissenschaften*. VS Verlag für Sozialwissenschaften. https://doi.org/10.1007/978-3-663-09682-5

Hagendorff, T. (2022). A virtue-based framework to support putting AI ethics into practice. *Philosophy and Technology, 35*(3), 55.

Nida-Rümelin, J. (1999). Zur Rolle ethischer Expertise in Projekten der Technikfolgenabschätzung. In *Angewandte Ethik in der pluralistischen Gesellschaft*. Universitätsverlag Freiburg Schweiz.

Palm, E., & Hansson, S. O. (2006). The case for ethical technology assessment (eTA). *Technological Forecasting and Social Change, 73*(5), 543–558. https://doi.org/10.1016/j.techfore.2005.06.002

Plato. (399 B.C.E.). Crito 48b. In A. Bailey (Ed.). (2024). *Socratic dialogues: Meno, Euthyphro, Apology, Crito, Phaedo* (C. Woods & R. Pack, Trans.). Broadview Press.

Smith, A. (1759). *A theory of moral sentiment*.

Stahl, B., Timmermans, J., & Mittelstadt, B. (2016). The ethics of computing. *ACM Computing Surveys, 48*, 1–38. https://doi.org/10.1145/2871196

Vallor, S., & Narayanan, A. (2021). *An introduction to software engineering ethics*. Retrieved from https://www.scu.edu/media/ethics-center/technology-ethics/Students.pdf

Vallor, S. (2016). Technology and the virtues: *A philosophical guide to a future worth wanting*. Oxford University Press.

van den Burg, S., & Swierstra, T. E. (2013). *Ethics on the laboratory floor*. Palgrave.

Wespire. (2020). *15 Insights into Gen Z, purpose, and the future of work*. Retrieved from https://www.wespire.com/15-insights-gen-z-purpose-and-future-of-work/

Winter, S. J., & Butler, B. S. (2021). Responsible technology design: Conversations for success. In *Perspectives on digital humanism* (pp. 271–275). Springer International Publishing.

Wright, D. (2011). A framework for the ethical impact assessment of information technology. *Ethics and Information Technology, 13*(3), 199–226. https://doi.org/10.1007/s10676-010-9242-6

Zuber, N., Gogoll, J., Kacianka, S., Nida-Rümelin, J., & Pretschner, A. (2024). Value-sensitive software design: Ethical deliberation in agile development processes. In H. Werthner, C. Ghezzi, J. Kramer, J. Nida-Rümelin, B. Nuseibeh, E. Prem, & A. Stanger (Eds.), *Introduction to digital humanism: A textbook* (p. 637). Springer Nature.

Open Access This chapter is licensed under the terms of the Creative Commons Attribution 4.0 International License (http://creativecommons.org/licenses/by/4.0/), which permits use, sharing, adaptation, distribution and reproduction in any medium or format, as long as you give appropriate credit to the original author(s) and the source, provide a link to the Creative Commons license and indicate if changes were made.

The images or other third party material in this chapter are included in the chapter's Creative Commons license, unless indicated otherwise in a credit line to the material. If material is not included in the chapter's Creative Commons license and your intended use is not permitted by statutory regulation or exceeds the permitted use, you will need to obtain permission directly from the copyright holder.

Chapter 4
What Is Ethics?

> "I want to discuss some problems created by a disparity between the fragmentation of value and the singleness of decision."
>
> Thomas Nagel, Mortal Question

Abstract This chapter introduces the foundational concepts of ethics and explores their relevance for software development. It distinguishes between descriptive, normative, and meta-ethics and offers an overview of key ethical theories, including deontology, consequentialism, virtue ethics, and contractualism. Rather than prescribing a single moral framework, the chapter embraces ethical pluralism, emphasizing the importance of deliberative judgment and context-sensitive reasoning in addressing moral challenges in software engineering. The chapter further examines the role of values, virtues, and attitudes, arguing that ethical reflection must extend beyond rules or outcomes to encompass the character and intentions of developers and organizations. It critiques common misconceptions—such as moral relativism, solutionism, and technical determinism—and frames ethics as a proactive, practice-oriented endeavor. Building on this foundation, the chapter outlines the distinction between applied and domain-specific ethics, demonstrating why software ethics must be understood as its own normative field shaped by the specific characteristics of digital technologies.

As the title of this book suggests, *Introduction to Ethical Software Development* tackles the ethical challenges that software developers and managers face in their work. Before diving into the specifics of ethical software development, it is crucial to establish a clear understanding of what ethics is actually about. While this might seem like an obvious requirement, it's far from simple due to the inherent complexity and confusion surrounding terms like "ethics," "morality," "value," "normativity," and "ought." We aim to guide you through the various demands often associated with ethical software development and address some of the common misconceptions we've encountered in our work with engineers, developers, and management.

In the realm of software development, the confusion is compounded by the multitude of demands placed on technology. Not only are engineers and designers expected to create software that is technologically reliable, secure, user-friendly, and morally desirable, but they must also ensure that it is quick to market and affordable. What all these demands have in common is a form of *imperative*: a specific outcome must be achieved—the products must meet certain criteria. Thus, these demands are **normative** in nature. These types of normative requirements fall within the realm of ethics: here, we scientifically discuss how human actions ought to fulfill certain norms and how we justify these norms. It is, therefore, a systematizing endeavor aimed at organizing actions, emotions, thoughts, and feelings in a normative way. It raises questions such as: Are these norms legitimate? If so, why? And if not, what are the alternatives? These pressures often fall on professionals who lack formal training in ethics and may find themselves grappling with unfamiliar concepts and difficult decisions.

When motivated engineers attempt to engage with ethical concerns, they frequently encounter overwhelming literature. Organizational value statements and codes of conduct, for instance, may leave engineers questioning the origin of these values, how to prioritize them in cases of conflict, and when or if they apply to the specific software they are developing. This can lead to frustration and a perception that ethical discussions are detached from the practical realities of software engineering. Even more so since the empirical turn in technology ethics, a plethora of individual case studies has emerged without proper systematization or categorization. This lack of theory makes it difficult to extract lessons learned, as no comprehensive framework is established to guide the analysis.

Ethics also plays a critical role in challenging both solutionism and technical determinism, which is the belief that technical solutions are inherently the best way to solve problems or that technology develops according to an unstoppable logic that leaves us with no real choice. Just because a technology that works as intended does not mean we are obligated to adopt it. Instead of merely asking what technology can do, we must ask whether it ought to be used, whether it is justifiable, acceptable, or desirable for individuals, communities, or society at large. The same ethical scrutiny applies to the opposite stance, often referred to as neo-Luddism, which views technology predominantly as a harmful or corrupting force. Ethics can provide the tools to evaluate this position as well, helping us recognize when technology genuinely contributes to normatively valuable goals. In this way, ethics navigates between uncritical enthusiasm and blanket rejection, fostering a thoughtful engagement with technological development. These questions open the door to morality, asking whether certain actions or behaviors infringe upon the freedoms and rights of others. This raises broader questions about how we want to live our lives and what kind of life we consider morally desirable.

A common misconception is that ethics is intangible and subjective, with arguments based solely on feelings or intuition, making it unpromising to navigate questions like whether privacy should be valued more than security or autonomy more than justice. However, ethics is more than a set of arbitrary preferences. Just as we consider certain physical facts about the world, such as the constitution of a rock, as objective, we also treat moral facts, like the wrongness of murder, as objective and binding. As Reid Blackman aptly puts it, "When people say ethics is squishy, they're effectively saying that they're not quite sure how to think about it, and they usually give up trying" (Blackman, 2022). This sentiment highlights the challenge of engaging with ethical questions, particularly in the context of software development. There is often a misconception that ethical thought is fundamentally different from a hard science like computer science, with a false dichotomy suggesting that the latter deals with truth and objectivity, while the former is based on feelings and subjectivity, both being somewhat arbitrary. However, this perception is far from accurate. Moral philosophy and ethics are grounded in reason and oriented toward empirically validated facts. While ethics necessarily involves human actors who have emotions and can be influenced or deceived, this does not render it subjective, arbitrary, or less rigorous than any other field of study. Normativity arises from our daily interactions and expectations we have toward each other. These rules constitute our societies, and if we do not follow or even break some of these rules, we may be prosecuted or cause moral outrage. They constitute our societies in the form of the basic law or human rights or as conventions and moral rules. The negotiation and interpretation of these determine our cultural identity.

The debate about whether IT requires its own unique ethics or whether existing moral principles can be applied to digital contexts is ongoing. However, the nature of moral claims does not fundamentally change when applied to software. For example, stealing a bike and copying proprietary software are both considered theft and as such legally punishable and morally reprehensible, even though the latter allows the original user to retain access to the software, whereas the former is left bikeless.

In this chapter, our goal is to provide a guiding thread through the maze of normative ethics in IT. While we may not provide definitive answers to specific ethical questions, we aim to equip development teams with the tools to navigate the complex landscape of ethics as they design and develop digital artifacts. Have no fear: as the Kantian adage *sapere aude* (loosely translated as *Have courage to use your own reason*) encourages everyone, ethics isn't reserved for an elite within an ivory tower; rather, it's a call to action for all of us to use our own mind and reason—something we already practice daily (Tasioulas, 2022).

4.1 Ethics as a Science

While information technology is unique in many ways, with an unmatched pace and scale of development, there's no need to reinvent the wheel by treating every ethical issue in software as entirely new or unprecedented. Philosophers, particularly in practical philosophy, have spent centuries and even millennia exploring concepts of normativity, duties, and consequences. We can draw on these established ideas, adapting and applying them to the specific challenges of software development.

Practical philosophy entails disciplines such as ethics, philosophy of law, philosophy of the state, political philosophy, and the foundations of economics. In contrast, the goal of theoretical philosophy is to understand the world and its objects. Unlike practical philosophy, it does not focus on how one should act but rather explores the question: What can I know? This book is not about that. Here, we aim to offer guidance for navigating ethical pressures, covering only as much ethical theory as necessary—no more. In the spirit of the quote attributed to Einstein, that everything should be made as simple as possible, but no simpler.

Practical philosophy is the institutionalized reflection that addresses central issues related to human actions, with a general claim to validity. This reflection occurs on three distinct levels: meta-theoretical, descriptive, and normative (Table 4.1). Through these levels, practical philosophy engages in a systematic examination of how we ought to act and the ethical implications of our choices. The meta-theoretical level addresses ethical concepts in order to develop scientific frameworks for engaging with questions of morality. It is thus the basis for descriptive and normative ethics. Descriptive ethics outlines the phenomenon of morality without itself making normative judgments. Normative ethics, on the other hand, formulates normative judgments about states of affairs and is therefore not neutral. Thus, as individual ethics, it discusses the principles of a morally conforming way of life, as political ethics the ideal of a just society or in digital ethics the attitude toward the development and use of digital technologies in the field of applied ethics.

In normative ethics, justifications are often grounded in fundamental ethical principles. These principles are supposed to guide individual actions and are typically categorized into four main types: deontological, consequentialist, contractualist, and virtue-ethical. The first three ethical theories integrate moral beliefs and apply a unified criterion to evaluate moral propositions. For instance, consequentialist principles assess actions based on their outcomes, while deontological principles emphasize duties and rules. Contractualist principles prioritize agreement and consent, both actual and hypothetical. These principles help normative ethics organize moral arguments into a coherent system. Nevertheless, no single ethical principle can fully account for all the reasons that guide our daily actions leading to a pluralist approach. Alternatively, virtue ethics focuses on character traits and how they shape moral behavior and decision-making. In contrast to consequentialism and deontology, virtue ethics is not centered around a specific rational principle that can be applied to a situation to determine whether it is morally appropriate. Instead, morality is about cultivating character traits (e.g., courage, kindness) that are considered

Table 4.1 Key differences between meta-ethics, descriptive ethics, and normative ethics

Aspect	Meta-ethics	Descriptive ethics	Normative ethics
Definition	Examines the nature of moral judgments and ethical language (e.g., what does "good" mean?)	Studies people's actual beliefs and behaviors related to ethics without making judgments	Explores what people *ought* to do; establishes principles for determining right from wrong
Focus	Nature and meaning of ethical terms, concepts, and moral reasoning	Describes and observes ethical practices, beliefs, and values within different societies and groups	Establishes and defends moral rules; developing moral principles that are aimed to directly guide human actions
Application in ethics	Forms the basis for understanding the foundational assumptions in ethical discussions	Provides insight into societal values, moral diversity, and how ethical norms are applied in real life	Guides decision-making in applied ethics, helping people determine "right" actions in fields like medicine, law, or tech

morally praiseworthy and living a life that embodies these virtues. The right action is one that a virtuous person would do naturally, without constant reasoning. Rather than following a strict rule, a virtuous person would tell the truth out of honesty, not because of a duty or potential outcome. This way, we do not need to engage in reasoning about the rightness of an action every time we encounter a moral conflict.

Moral conflicts or even moral dilemmas arise because we live in a pluralistic society, where our actions are often justified by a variety of factors, including social norms, obligations, roles, and principles or values. Each of these can serve as valid moral reasons, but they can also come into conflict, as is frequently the case (in fact, if they wouldn't, ethics would be a boring, albeit easier endeavor) (Table 4.2). Therefore, it is crucial to emphasize the importance of judgment and the ability to deliberate. Critical thinking, and more specifically, moral reasoning, involves carefully assessing the validity of moral arguments. In applied ethics, we try to evaluate the coherence of individual decisions, statements, or actions with respect to a specific domain. With this foundation in mind, let's explore and systematize the four core ethical theories.

4.1.1 Consequentialism

Consequentialist ethics judge the morality of an action based on its consequences. This ethical theory posits that the ultimate basis for determining the rightness or wrongness of conduct lies in the outcomes it produces. From a consequentialist

Table 4.2 Comparative overview of consequentialism, deontology, virtue ethics, and contractualism

Aspect	Consequentialism	Deontology	Virtue ethics	Contractualism
Definition	Ethical theory that determines the rightness of actions based on their outcomes or consequences	Ethical theory that focuses on duties and rules; the morality of an action is based on adherence to these rules	Ethical theory that emphasizes the development of virtuous character traits as the basis of moral behavior	Ethical theory that determines right and wrong based on principles of mutual agreement or social contracts
Key questions	What outcome will bring the most good or least harm?	What is my duty or obligation in this situation?	What kind of person should I be?	Could all reasonable people agree to this principle?
Focus	The consequences or results of actions	Adherence to moral rules, duties, or obligations	The character and virtues of the individual	Fairness, mutual respect, and principles everyone would accept as fair
Moral basis	Good actions are those that lead to the best overall consequences	Right actions are those that follow moral rules or duties	Right actions stem from a person's virtues and character	Right actions are those that could be agreed upon by all as fair and just

standpoint, a morally right action—or even the decision not to act—is one that results in a favorable outcome, that is, the action produces something that is, on balance, better than any alternative.

Consequentialism is part of the broader category of teleological ethics (from the Greek telos = end, goal), which includes various views that claim the moral value of any action is rooted in its tendency to produce desirable outcomes. Consequentialists generally believe that an action is right if, and only if, it produces, is likely to produce, or is intended to produce a greater balance of good over evil than any other available alternative. This approach emphasizes the importance of considering the potential benefits and harms of different actions to ensure that the best possible outcome is achieved. Of course, to maximize what is considered good, one must first define what "good" and "bad" mean. This is no simple task. An obvious way is to refer to pain and pleasure as Jeremy Bentham (1973/2007) famously did: "Nature has placed mankind under the governance of two sovereign masters, pain and pleasure. It is for them alone to point out what we ought to do, as well as to determine what we shall do." In Bentham's view, happiness is achieved by maximizing pleasure and minimizing pain. He is a proponent of *utilitarianism*, a well-known form of consequentialism, which argues that an action is morally right if it generates the greatest happiness for the greatest number of people. In practice, this means that a decision would be considered morally good if it either reduces the overall amount of pain, increases pleasure, or achieves an optimal balance between the two, where improving one does not worsen the other.

In addition to determining the nature of what we consider "good" and "bad" that should be maximized, another critical issue is the scope of the consequences we evaluate. It's important to consider not only the immediate outcomes of an action but also its indirect effects, long-term results, and potential side effects. This challenge becomes even more complex with the advent of new technologies, as unintended consequences are often difficult to predict.

Like other ethical theories, consequentialism requires the consideration of various factors. Here, the core focus is on the consequences of the action, which must be carefully evaluated. Understanding this theory allows us to critically assess the potential outcomes of our decisions, ensuring they align with our ethical goals.

4.1.2 Deontology

Deontological ethics, derived from the Greek word *deon*, meaning duty, is an ethical framework that emphasizes the intrinsic morality of actions, independent of their consequences. Unlike consequentialist theories, deontological ethics asserts that certain actions are morally required or forbidden based on a set of rules or duties.

One of the most influential figures in deontological ethics is Immanuel Kant (1785/2013), who introduced the concept of the categorical imperative. Kant argued that we should act according to maxims, that is, a subjective principle of action, that we would want to become universal laws. In other words, one should only act in a way that could be consistently applied as a universal rule for everyone.

A prominent example is the case of lying. According to deontological principles, lying is inherently wrong because if everyone lied, trust and communication would break down, making social interactions impossible. Even if a lie might have positive outcomes, such as sparing someone's feelings, deontological ethics would still consider it morally wrong because it violates the duty to be truthful.

Another classic example is the duty to keep promises. Imagine you promised a friend to help them move into their new house on Saturday. On that day, you receive an invitation to a highly anticipated event that you've been eager to attend. From a deontological perspective, you are morally obligated to keep your promise and help your friend, despite the tempting alternative. This is because the duty to honor promises is considered morally binding, regardless of the personal consequences.

Deontological ethics also encompasses rights-based theories, where individuals have certain inviolable rights. For instance, the right to life or freedom is viewed as absolute, and any action that violates these rights is deemed unethical, regardless of the outcomes that might justify such actions from a consequentialist perspective.

The central criterion in deontological ethics is *duty*. Actions are evaluated based on whether they align with moral duties, principles, or rules, such as honesty, fairness, or respect for others. This framework upholds the idea that some actions are inherently right or wrong, independent of the consequences they produce. By focusing on duties and principles, deontological ethics provides a clear, rule-based approach to moral decision-making, emphasizing the importance of acting consistently with ethical principles. However, there are often situations where two or more principles conflict, requiring us to evaluate which duty or right takes precedence in that particular case. It's crucial to recognize that, even in such conflicts, deontological ethics dismisses outcomes as irrelevant; they are not considered significant enough to override established duties and rights.

4.1.3 Virtue Ethics

Virtue ethics does not center its approach on outcomes or rules. Instead, it highlights the significance of virtues and practical wisdom (phronesis), which are intimately linked. Virtues are not simply habits; they are deeply rooted character traits or dispositions that define a person's identity. These traits are deliberately cultivated, not developed accidentally or unintentionally.

A virtuous person does not need to evaluate every situation from the ground up to determine the right course of action; their behavior naturally stems from their virtues. For instance, a just individual is not someone who practices justice, such as distributing resources equally. If their actions are driven by self-interest, fear of repercussions, or the belief that justice is merely a practical policy, they are not acting with true virtue. True justice must be valued for its own sake, independent of external motives.

This distinction gives rise to a classification of three types of individuals: the strong-willed, the abstinent, and the virtuous. The virtuous person acts justly because they genuinely value justice, free from internal conflict or competing desires. In contrast to the strong-willed or abstinent person, who may grapple with contrary urges, the virtuous individual acts in alignment with their character. For example, virtues like honesty and courage are not merely about following rules but reflect the expression of deeply embedded character traits.

However, having virtues alone may not be enough to navigate the complexities of moral life, especially in nuanced situations. It can seem paradoxical that justice, friendship, honesty, compassion, and courage—though virtues—can sometimes be faults. A compassionate or courageous person may not always be morally good, or if we assume these traits inherently make someone good, they could occasionally lead the person to act wrongly. This appears contradictory. This is where phronesis or practical wisdom becomes essential. Phronesis equips individuals with the ability to reason and apply their virtues appropriately in different contexts, helping them confront moral challenges thoughtfully and effectively.

In everyday use, or when motivation is driven by inclination, we arrive at what Aristotle (350 BC/ 2014) termed "natural virtue"—a preliminary stage of full virtue that awaits completion through phronesis or practical wisdom. Without insight, there can be no complete virtue. While children may display these inclinations, they are not fully virtuous, as they lack the wisdom that comes with phronesis.

Generally, good intentions aim to act rightly or "do the right thing," and practical wisdom provides the knowledge or understanding that enables its possessor—unlike well-intentioned but inexperienced individuals—to do so in any given situation.

Hence, two crucial aspects of practical wisdom become evident. First, it typically develops through life experience. Second, a practically wise person can identify which aspects of a situation are the most important or, in some cases, the only relevant ones. These cultivated human abilities help resolve moral conflicts and overcome ignorance.

4.1.4 Contractualist Ethics

Contractualist ethics is centered around the idea that moral principles are justified through mutual agreement or consent, whether actual or hypothetical. This theory suggests that what is morally right is based on the terms of a "social contract" that rational individuals would agree upon if they were all treated as equals and were seeking fair terms of cooperation.

The origins of contractualist thought can be traced back to philosophers like Thomas Hobbes, John Locke, and Jean-Jacques Rousseau, but it was more recently refined by John Rawls and James Buchanan. According to John Rawls (1971), in his seminal work *A Theory of Justice*, individuals should determine the principles of justice from an *original position* behind a *veil of ignorance*. This hypothetical scenario requires individuals to choose the rules for society without knowing their own status, wealth, abilities, or preferences, ensuring that the principles selected would be fair and just for all.

For example, consider the principle of equal rights. From a contractualist perspective, people behind the veil of ignorance would likely agree that everyone should have the same basic rights, such as freedom of speech or the right to personal safety, since no one knows in advance which position they would occupy in society. This agreement forms the foundation of moral obligations and societal norms that are seen as fair and just.

In his influential work *The Calculus of Consent*, Buchanan (1965) argued that just as markets work through voluntary exchange, political decisions should also be viewed as a form of collective agreement or contract among individuals. According to Buchanan, a legitimate government is one that operates based on rules and policies that individuals would agree to under conditions of fairness and rational deliberation. He emphasized that individuals should be viewed as rational agents who enter into agreements to form the rules and structures that govern society, much like they would enter into contracts in a market. Buchanan's approach highlights the importance of *voluntary consent* and *mutual benefit* in creating ethical and political systems. He argued that rules should be evaluated based on whether free and rational individuals would agree to them and that political structures should be designed to reflect the genuine preferences and choices of individuals, rather than being imposed by an external authority.

The criterion in contractualist ethics is thus *agreement* or *consent*. It emphasizes that moral principles should be those that rational individuals would agree to if they were in a position to deliberate freely, fairly, and without coercion. This focus on mutual agreement respects the autonomy and rationality of individuals, ensuring that ethical principles are rooted in fairness, reciprocity, and respect for others' interests.

An everyday example of contractualist thinking is found in societal laws and regulations. When we follow traffic rules, pay taxes, or adhere to social norms, we are essentially participating in a social contract that maintains order and fairness in society. We abide by these rules not because of immediate consequences but because, as a collective, we agree that such rules are essential for a functioning community.

To illustrate the differing perspectives of ethical theories, consider the following scenario (Table 4.3): A developer discovers a potentially dangerous bug in her company's software. She could disclose and fix it immediately by pushing an urgent update resolving the issue quickly but potentially damaging the company's reputation and eroding user trust. Alternatively, she could wait for the next scheduled update to quietly include the fix, thereby avoiding public scrutiny but leaving users exposed to potential harm in the meantime. The following table simplifies the situation to highlight the contrasting ethical approaches; in reality, additional factors such as legal obligations and organizational policies would also play a role.

Table 4.3 Applying ethical theories to real-world scenarios

Ethical theory	Potential application to the scenario
Consequentialism	Disclose the vulnerability if doing so results in the **best overall outcome**—minimizing harm to users, perhaps by patching it quickly and notifying users in a way that prevents exploitation
Deontology	Disclose the vulnerability immediately because honesty and duty to protect users are **moral obligations**, regardless of reputational consequences
Virtue ethics	A virtuous developer **acts with integrity and courage**, disclosing the issue out of moral character and care for users, rather than rule-following or fear of consequences
Contractualism	Disclose the vulnerability through a process that rational, fair-minded individuals (users, developers, stakeholders) would agree to—like responsible and timely disclosure protocols

4.2 From Applied Ethics to Domain Ethics

The ethical theories under consideration claim universal scope, offering principles meant to apply no matter the circumstances or the particular form an action takes. Thus, the ethical value of an action is not determined by its context but by the underlying moral principles. Immanuel Kant would argue that even if lying might lead to a better outcome (e.g., protecting your friend), it is still morally wrong because it violates the duty to be truthful. This is because the ethical value of the act lies in the act itself, not in the results it produces. While deontological or consequentialist ethics emphasize the importance of acting according to universal moral principles, real-life situations often involve complex emotional and relational considerations. Very often, our actions are guided by more than a single moral principle. Strictly adhering to duty without regard for context can sometimes lead to moral dilemmas and strained relationships. For instance, if you always prioritize telling the truth over protecting a friend in need, you risk damaging the trust and emotional bond that form the basis of meaningful human connections. This tension between principle and practical human experience highlights why many philosophers, like Aristotle with his virtue ethics or contemporary ethicists advocating for care ethics, argue for a more context-sensitive approach that considers the emotions, relationships, and well-being of those involved.

Each of the major ethical theories is perfectly rational on its own. Deontology is compelling because motives and duties *do* seem central to moral judgment; consequentialism is just as persuasive because results clearly matter; and theories that foreground consent or moral character also resonate with our intuitions. Yet the guidance these systems offer frequently clashes: what duty requires, a utilitarian calculus may forbid, and a virtue-based view may evaluate differently still. How, then, do we steer through a moral landscape where equally reasonable theories pull us toward incompatible actions?

Thomas Nagel (1979) discusses the complexity of our moral real life in his famous essay, *The Fragmentation of Value*. The real world is characterized by the coexistence of conflicting yet equally valid values, which often resist reduction to a single, unified moral perspective. This pluralism means that individuals and societies must navigate moral landscapes where trade-offs are inevitable and no single principle can universally resolve all dilemmas. He distinguishes between personal values such as love, loyalty, and individual commitments and impersonal moral values like justice and impartial concern for others. He further separates agent-relative reasons, tied to one's specific roles or relationships, from agent-neutral reasons that apply universally. Nagel emphasizes the tension between the individual perspective and the detached *view from nowhere*, arguing that these different standpoints generate genuine moral conflicts that cannot always be resolved through a single ethical theory. Similarly, John Rawls called this clash of reasonable outlooks the *burdens of judgment*: "a plurality of reasonable, yet incompatible, comprehensive doctrines is the normal result of the exercise of human reason within the framework of the free institutions of a constitutional democratic regime" (Rawls, 1971). People reasonably disagree because of several factors, among them the complexity of evidence, which individuals may interpret differently, and the influence of diverse and idiosyncratic life experiences that shape values and perspectives of individuals. People also prioritize values—such as liberty, equality, or tradition—in different ways. Finally, human reasoning itself is limited (or bounded as economists would call it) and shaped by social and cultural backgrounds, making disagreement even among well-intentioned and rational individuals inevitable.

We may converge on high-level principles of justice, but when competing values meet concrete situations, agreement often fades. It is easier to agree on the statement "Humans shall be free" than it is to agree on the exact policy regarding free speech and hate speech or discrimination, etc. Ambiguity, then, is not a temporary lapse in reasoning; it is a structural feature of moral life in a pluralistic society. We must navigate it even when equally credible theories tug us toward incompatible actions.

This is a critical observation, as many social domains such as medicine, friendship, and technology frequently involve a spectrum of actions that cannot be explained and justified by one ethical theory. In these contexts, moral decision-making cannot rely on a one-size-fits-all approach. Instead, it demands a nuanced deliberation that recognizes the interplay of multiple, sometimes conflicting, values and principles, as well as the importance of situational and relational factors. Acknowledging this pluralism helps avoid moral oversimplification and allows for more context-sensitive ethical reasoning. In the following, we will briefly outline that applying ethical principles to individual cases may be insufficient, and thus, sometimes, a domain of human practice may require its own idiosyncratic domain ethics.

4.2.1 Applied Ethics

How, then, do we bridge the gap between lofty ethical theories and the down-to-earth question of what action to take in this domain-specific situation? It is crucial to understand that social domains can be sufficiently unique to warrant their own form of ethical reasoning. In such cases, the domain itself gives rise to a distinct ethical approach, shaped by its particular characteristics and demands. In (scientific) ethics, the first attempt is the application of ethical theories to concrete situations, which is why it is called applied ethics. It is usually understood as the application of abovementioned ethical principles to specific domains, such as medicine, bioethics (including issues like treatment of embryos and abortion), or environmental and animal ethics, which expand the traditional focus of ethical reflection beyond human relationships. Within these domains, ethical theories are used to evaluate decisions, emphasizing either the duties and obligations relevant to that context or the careful weighing of potential consequences. Or, as in our case, technology ethics, which examines the ethical implications of technological innovation and its impact on individuals, relationships, and society.

However, this is a top-down academic approach that applies ethical theories to real-life situations. But real life does not always match these theories. We do not always make decisions strictly in line with ethical theories. If we did, it would often lead to moral distress, as illustrated by the earlier example of the trade-off between duty and friendship. Sometimes, the theories themselves need to change, e.g., Skorupinski and Ott (2000) point out that using general moral rules, like the rule against killing, in complex systems like transportation is not easy. If we applied that rule strictly, most modern transport would seem morally unacceptable. This issue becomes especially clear in the debate around autonomous cars, where it is clear that accidents will still happen, even with the best technology (Gogoll & Müller, 2017).

This shows a major challenge in applied ethics. Traditionally, applied ethics tries to organize and explain moral beliefs using ethical principles (Nida-Rümelin, 2005). But unlike this classical approach, many real-world problems need more flexible thinking. In these cases, it is the practical problems themselves that shape ethical thinking. They become the starting point for developing ethical ideas. For this reason, we speak not of applied ethics but of ethics specific to a given domain.

4.2.2 Domain-Specific Ethics

Nida-Rümelin (2005) argues that the dominant paradigms in modern ethics are often too simplistic to capture the full range of real-life situations. This is why domain-specific ethics have emerged. Unlike applied ethics, which focuses on applying general moral principles, domain-specific ethics are deeply embedded in specific social contexts and practices. They draw on the insights of various disciplines and professions to address complex, context-dependent ethical challenges (Nida-Rümelin, 2005). These approaches take into account the normative structures and practices within these contexts, recognizing that ethical judgment is not just about applying abstract principles but also about understanding the evolving norms that guide human action in specific fields (Table 4.4).

For example, healthcare ethics focuses on the values of healing and care, while business ethics is concerned with fair distribution of resources. Each field has its own core values that guide ethical decision-making, which means that ethical demands and considerations vary significantly across different domains. In this sense, domain-specific ethics can be seen as an ethical inquiry into societal subsystems, each defined by its own purpose and normative framework.

Technology ethics, in particular, presents a unique challenge. In contrast to domains like medicine, which revolve around a clearly defined social aim (e.g., healing), technology ethics must grapple with the dual challenge of assessing the nature of digital artifacts and understanding their varied impacts across different social subsystems and user roles. This has given rise to a variety of technology ethics within the context of digitality such as information ethics, computer ethics, AI ethics, digital ethics, and others. Each of these addresses a specific form of ethical inquiry, shaped either by the technological nature of the systems involved or by the particular social contexts in which they operate.

As Saetra and Danaher (2022) point out, this proliferation of domain-specific ethics within technology ethics can lead to fragmentation and unnecessary duplication of effort, potentially wasting resources and reducing the clarity of ethical analysis. They argue for a more unified approach to ethics that can address the broad range of digital phenomena. However, we contend that it is still essential to

Table 4.4 Applied ethics versus domain-specific ethics

	Applied ethics	**Domain-specific ethics**
Main difference	Starts with *general* moral theories or broad principles and **applies** them to a concrete case	Starts with the *practice itself*—its goals, norms, workflows, risks, etc.—and tries to **extract** ethical guidance from within
Example question	"Given this theory, what should clinicians/engineers/teachers/lawyers do in this particular situation?"	"Given what we actually do in this domain, what values, duties, and trade-offs emerge? And how can we act right?"
Specific context	Context *supplies cases* that existing theories are applied to	Context is *constitutive*: values often make sense *only* inside that ecosystem (e.g., *maintainability* in software, *informed consent* in medicine)
Approach	Top-down, deductive or principlist; often framed as applications of deontological or utilitarian theories	Bottom-up, interpretive, interdisciplinary; blends empirical studies, design probes, professional norms, and sometimes local regulations
Potential risk	Risk of *over-universalising*: may miss tacit know-how or power asymmetries inside the subfield	Risk of *fragmentation*: dozens of micro-ethics subfields can create silos, duplication of effort, or inconsistent standards

recognize the unique nature of digital technologies and the distinct ethical issues they raise. We believe that a balanced approach is necessary: one that combines a broad understanding of technology's general ethical issues with a more focused, theoretically grounded exploration of its specific challenges.

Therefore, we will use the term "domain-specific ethics" to refer to these more context-dependent approaches to ethics in practice. This reflects our understanding that ethical reflection must consider both the unique characteristics of digital technologies and the broader, interdisciplinary frameworks within which they are embedded. This combination allows for a more precise and contextually relevant ethical analysis, ensuring that technology ethics remains both rigorous and practically applicable. This goes hand in hand with a more bottom-up approach to scientific ethics, one that allows for a variety of actions and a pluralism of legitimate values, without reducing ethics to mere acceptance of what people happen to consider legitimate. Rather, it follows a line of reasoning grounded in pre-theoretical or common-sense moral intuitions.

4.3 Conclusion

Ethical theories are particularly useful when we need clear guidance and scientific theories for making moral decisions. They help us identify a "case for ethics," that is, the ethical significance of certain situations or technologies. A good example of this is the IEEE 7000 approach, which seeks to systematically integrate ethical considerations into technology development by translating concrete ethical principles and values like fairness, transparency, and accountability into technical standards.

Additionally, ethical theories serve as deliberation tools, enabling us to evaluate actions and decisions. They provide theories like utilitarianism or deontology that help analyze the moral consequences of actions or weigh duties and rights. These theories not only answer the question "What should I do?" but also "Why is one action morally better than another?"

Ethical theories are more than just abstract concepts. They are essential tools for understanding, evaluating, and justifying the moral dimensions of decisions. They offer guidance in identifying ethically relevant situations, reflecting on values, and making moral judgments. In a world where technological advancements increasingly raise complex ethical questions, ethical theories are a necessary toolkit for making responsible decisions and building trust in technological innovation.

In the next chapter, we highlight a central function of ethical theories, that is, their role as a moral compass. Values are fundamental beliefs about what is considered important and right in a society or specific context. They provide guidance in complex, often-conflicting decision-making situations by defining the foundational goals and priorities of an ethical system. For instance, a value like autonomy emphasizes the importance of personal freedom and self-determination, while justice focuses on fairness and equal rights.

References

Aristotle (ca. 350 BC/2014) Crisp, R. (Ed.). Aristotle: nicomachean ethics. Cambridge University Press.
Bentham, J. (1973/2007). Principles of morals and legislation. *Dover Publications Inc.*
Blackman, R. (2022). *Ethical machines: Your concise guide to totally unbiased, transparent, and respectful AI*. Harvard Business Press.
Buchanan, J. M., & Tullock, G. (1965). The calculus of consent: Logical foundations of constitutional democracy (Vol. 100). University of Michigan press.
Gogoll, J., & Müller, J. F. (2017). Autonomous cars: In favor of a mandatory ethics setting. *Science and Engineering Ethics, 23*(3), 681 700.
Kant, I. (1785/2013). Moral law: Groundwork of the metaphysics of morals. Routledge.
Nagel, T. (1979). *Mortal questions*. Cambridge University Press.
Nida-Rümelin, J. (2005). *Angewandte Ethik: Die Bereichsethiken und ihre theoretische Fundierung; ein Handbuch*. Kröner.
Sætra, H. S., & Danaher, J. (2022). To each technology its own ethics: The problem of ethical proliferation. *Philosophy and Technology, 35*(4), 93.
Skorupinski, B., & Ott, K. (2000). Technikfolgenabschätzung und Ethik. Eine Verhältnisbestimmung in Theorie und Praxis. *TATuP—Zeitschrift für Technikfolgenabschätzung in Theorie Und Praxis, 9*(2), 98–102.
Rawls, J. (1971/2005). A theory of justice. Harvard University Press.
Tasioulas, J. (2022). Artificial intelligence, humanistic ethics. *Daedalus, 151*(2), 232–243.

Open Access   This chapter is licensed under the terms of the Creative Commons Attribution 4.0 International License (http://creativecommons.org/licenses/by/4.0/), which permits use, sharing, adaptation, distribution and reproduction in any medium or format, as long as you give appropriate credit to the original author(s) and the source, provide a link to the Creative Commons license and indicate if changes were made.

The images or other third party material in this chapter are included in the chapter's Creative Commons license, unless indicated otherwise in a credit line to the material. If material is not included in the chapter's Creative Commons license and your intended use is not permitted by statutory regulation or exceeds the permitted use, you will need to obtain permission directly from the copyright holder.

Chapter 5
Values and Software

> *"Valuing is creating: hear it, ye creating ones! Valuation itself is the treasure and jewel of the valued things. Through valuation only is there value; and without valuation the nut of existence would be hollow. Hear it, ye creating ones!"*
>
> Friedrich Nietzsche—*Thus spoke Zarathustra*

Abstract This chapter explores the central role of values in ethical software development discussions. As the discourse in AI and digital ethics has shifted from abstract moral theory to a value-centric vocabulary, values such as fairness, privacy, and transparency have become common currency among engineers, regulators, and the public. Yet the flexibility of the term *value* also presents philosophical and practical challenges. Drawing on ethics, philosophy of technology, and software engineering, this chapter examines how values can guide ethical reflection, design, and implementation. We distinguish between techno-generic values—those inherent to the nature of digital technologies—and domain-specific values rooted in the social contexts in which systems are deployed. By introducing a triadic model of ethical design—comprising identification, deliberation, and implementation—we offer a structured approach for integrating values into digital systems in a non-arbitrary, transparent, and context-sensitive manner. Ultimately, the chapter argues that values, properly understood and operationalized, serve not only as normative goals but also as epistemic tools to navigate ethical complexity in software systems.

5.1 Why Values Matter in Software Ethics

If you have read anything at all about ethics and software, you will have noticed an abundance of talk about *values*—from privacy and fairness to transparency and human autonomy. Yet in the broader history of moral philosophy, the concept of *values* itself has not typically taken center stage; classical theorists like Aristotle, Kant, or Mill focused more on virtues, duties, or the highest good. In debates about ethical software and AI, the discourse, however, has shifted decisively to a *value-centric* vocabulary—up to a point where there seems to be no merit in attempting to alter that development. Naturally, this led to more value-centric approaches focusing on specific values (such as privacy, fairness, or accountability) that technology should uphold, rather than on high-level theory. Essentially, as computing technologies began to deeply influence individual lives and societies, scholars and engineers started wondering what desirable values are at stake and how or if at all we can ensure that digital technology fosters those values. For example, instead of debating utilitarian vs. deontological ethics, conversations shifted to ensuring an AI system embodies values like fairness or transparency. This turn toward values made ethical discussions more accessible to designers, policymakers, and users. Therefore, this change can be largely attributed—at least in our opinion—to a pragmatic turn in both academic and industry discussions: identifying and specifying values offers a language that resonates with a wide array of stakeholders such as developers, regulators, executives, and users alike. Values thus become a kind of bridging concept also between disciplines: Values connect various disciplines by providing a shared language for discussing what is desired since they resonate across fields such as economics, sociology, and biology, each of which grapples with the question of what is seen as desirable or worth pursuing, albeit from distinct perspectives. In contrast, ethics is more prescriptive, concerned with what ought to be done, all things considered. By focusing on values, also software development practitioners can move toward one shared dialogue that bridges diverse design approaches, including Human-Computer Interaction (HCI), Value Sensitive Design (VSD), Participatory Design (PD), Universal Design (UD), User-Centered Design (UCD), and User Experience Design (UXD). Despite their varying methods and contexts, these approaches share a common commitment to enhancing values that go beyond mere technical functionality, focusing instead on creating systems that align with broader human needs and ethical considerations (Shilton, 2018). Regulators, companies, and the public might not all be moral philosophers, but terms like "privacy" or "safety" are widely understood and appreciated, or at least people *believe* they share the same understanding and appreciation. Focusing on values allows ethical goals to be communicated in a way that policymakers, companies, as well as engineers, or society at large, can engage with. Moreover, values are often seen as providing positive guidance for behavior, encouraging desirable actions and outcomes, rather than simply prohibiting certain conduct, as is typical in many ethical theories. Unlike the more rigid, rule-based nature of ethical theories, values foster a more flexible and constructive mindset, focusing on aspirations and ideals rather than merely avoiding wrongdoing.

The idea of value alignment that entails ensuring software systems act in accordance with values has since become a key topic also in AI research or AI ethics. By articulating specific values (like safety, fairness, human autonomy) as design goals, developers aim to prevent AI from causing value violations. In fact, numerous high-profile AI ethics initiatives have converged on a set of broadly accepted values. A 2019 analysis of 84 AI ethics guidelines found a striking convergence around about 8 key values including privacy, accountability, safety, transparency, fairness, human

5.1 Why Values Matter in Software Ethics

control, professional responsibility, and promotion of human values (Jobin et al., 2019). This shows that across different organizations and governments, there is a shared vocabulary of values deemed important for AI.

Even regulators and governments set the tone of the debate, and they also have chosen to emphasize ethical alignment. Governments and international organizations now explicitly weave values, principles, and requirements into their AI strategies. It advocates for developing AI in alignment with these values and proposes tools like Ethical Impact Assessments to gauge that alignment. This widespread call in policymaking for AI systems to respect our values highlights how crucial and prominent this approach has become. Although AI is but one aspect of the broader software sphere, it remains the prevailing focus in this space. UNESCO's 2021 Global Recommendation on the Ethics of AI emphasizes the protection of human rights and dignity, the promotion of diversity and inclusion, the fostering of just societies, and the commitment to environmental sustainability as foundational values. However, because values are often abstract and aspirational, they need to be translated into principles that can guide concrete actions. In the context of software systems, this means defining technical and accessible requirements that embody these values, ensuring they are meaningfully integrated into the design and operation of digital technologies. For instance, the European Union's High-Level Expert Group on AI (HLEG) released Ethics Guidelines for Trustworthy AI in 2019, anchored in four core ethical principles derived from European fundamental rights: respect for human autonomy, prevention of harm, fairness, and explicability. The EU guidelines then translate these principles into seven concrete technical requirements: human oversight, technical robustness, privacy and data governance, transparency, diversity/non-discrimination, societal and environmental well-being, and accountability (Table 5.1).

However, it can be challenging to determine which values to prioritize, how to identify them, and how to justify the selected values. Moreover, translating or deconstructing values into principles, then into requirements, and eventually into detailed specifications is far from straightforward. Numerous methods exist, reflecting the variety of disciplines attempting to address this complex challenge (Nyholm, 2022). Methods for the identification and legitimization of values are fundamentally a philosophical endeavor. At the same time, software engineering and the social sciences offer numerous approaches to understanding the social acceptance of certain values, as well as methods for interpreting, translating, and implementing them within engineering processes. For example, participatory design methods involve

Table 5.1 Values, principles, and requirements in software development

Values	Principles	Requirements
Privacy	Respect for human autonomy	Data governance
Accountability	Prevention of harm	Technical robustness and safety
Transparency	Explicability	Human oversight
Inclusivity	Fairness	Diversity and non-discrimination
Human control	Prevention of harm	Societal and environmental well-being

stakeholders early in the development process to ensure that their values and expectations are reflected in the system requirements. Similarly, techniques such as Value Sensitive Design (VSD) aim to systematically integrate moral values into the design of technology; for instance, the value of privacy can be translated into specific requirements such as data minimization, user consent mechanisms, and encryption protocols.

Most importantly, values need to be identified first before they can be interpreted, translated, or implemented. Without a clear understanding of which values are at stake, any attempt to design ethically responsible technology risks being arbitrary or incomplete. Doing so risks falling into the trap of ethical whitewashing, especially when we are not even certain about the nature of the values we are addressing. Thus, in this chapter, we will explore the nature of values and the challenges they present in the context of ethical software engineering.

5.2 Defining Values: Philosophical and Practical Dimensions

As mentioned above, one of the benefits of talking about values is that everyone assumes they understand the term, believe others share that understanding, and thus find the conversation straightforward. However, this apparent clarity has a downside: once we are required to spell out what we mean by values more concretely, we discover the notion is far less obvious than we initially assumed. So what do we really mean by values? Sometimes, we refer to values that have faded over time or no longer garner the same attention. We also invoke values when discussing democracy or health or when describing qualities that give something worth, such as the beauty of a tree, or when considering ends or objectives we deem desirable. We talk of valuations of goods and companies, as well as intrinsic values we see as inherently good. Still, the true nature of values remains elusive, and their *ontology*, as philosophers say, is not clearly defined: are they properties, goods, or principles that guide action?

The notion of value has deep roots in ethics (the use of value-centric vocabulary, however, has not). In classical philosophy, thinkers like Aristotle discussed in his *Nicomachean Ethics* (350 b.C.) the Good as the ultimate aim of human life, even if they did not use the modern term of values. Aristotle, for example, identified eudaimonia (flourishing) as the highest good pursued for its own sake and never merely as a means to something else. This foreshadows the important distinction between intrinsic and instrumental value. An intrinsic value is something valued in itself (an end in itself), whereas an instrumental value is valued as a means to an end. For instance, friendship is intrinsically worthwhile, while wealth or health was chiefly valuable as an instrument to achieve a long life.

But how can ethical theories help us understand values? Ethical theories provide insights into the origins and foundations of these values. However, they not only help us understand the source of values but also provide theories for identifying what is considered valuable. They guide us in evaluating actions, intentions, and outcomes, offering criteria to distinguish between mere preferences and moral principles. These theories also help clarify the broader context in which values arise, such as cultural, social, or professional norms, and provide a basis for justifying why certain values should be prioritized in specific situations.

Whether values are considered as properties, goods, or states or intentions depends on the ethical stance we are taking. Looking at the theories explained above, we can distinguish different opinions on the nature of values: Consequentialist theories focus on goods, meaning that what is considered valuable is a particular state of affairs or an external reality. In this view, ethical evaluation depends on the outcomes or consequences of actions, with value being attributed to, e.g., overall well-being, happiness, or other desired states that actions bring about. Thus, the worth of something is determined by its contribution to achieving a favorable or optimal outcome. John Stuart Mill (1863) famously argued that pleasure and the absence of pain are the only things desirable as ends. Thus, pleasure or happiness is the only value that matters, making classical utilitarianism a *monistic* theory. In deontological theories, value is found in principles, duties, or intentions. An action is valuable not because of its consequences but because it aligns with moral rules or duties, such as truthfulness, justice, or respect for human dignity and actions that coincide with those we refer to as valuable. Immanuel Kant (1797/2017), contrary to Mill, maintained that rational beings have intrinsic worth (dignity) and must therefore be treated as *ends in themselves*, never merely as means. Thus, Kant saw a *good will* and respect for persons as intrinsically good, while things like talent or intelligence had value only when aligned with good will. Virtue ethicists such as Aristotle (350 BC 2014) integrate both perspectives: they seek guiding principles for action while also emphasizing their embodiment in the world. Their focus is on cultivating valuable character traits that enable individuals to act virtuously. Hence, professional ethics align with this approach, as they emphasize attitudes that are desirable precisely because they foster ethically desirable actions. This is what codes of conduct address as desirable behavior among software engineers to foster ethical design and responsible decision-making. Unlike regulations and standards, which set enforceable product requirements, codes of conduct provide guiding principles and professional norms that encourage engineers to act ethically. They promote values such as honesty, fairness, responsibility, and respect for user rights. By shaping professional culture, codes of conduct help ensure that ethical considerations are not just external constraints but become intrinsic to the development process.

Additionally, we have a debate on value pluralism, i.e., that there are many values that are legitimated (Chap. 4). Value pluralism holds that there are multiple values like justice, freedom, and happiness, instead of a single supreme value. In contrast, value monists argue that all values can be traced back to a fundamental, singular value. As we have outlined, consequentialist theories often prioritize pleasure or well-being as the ultimate value, making them monistic. In such theories, friendship is regarded as merely an instrumental value for maximizing pleasure or well-being. Deontological approaches can be either monistic or pluralistic, depending on how many principles they consider relevant. The key issue is the number of principles involved. Additionally, *applied ethics* (such as bioethics, environmental ethics, business ethics) brought the language of values into practical debates. For example, environmental ethics argued for the intrinsic value of non-human life or ecosystems expanding the notion of value beyond human-centered terms.

When it comes to software engineering, we see pragmatic definitions: Van de Poel, for instance, defines values as "lasting convictions or matters that people feel should be strived for in general and not just for themselves to be able to lead a good life or realize a good society" (van de Poel, 2021). The IEEE standard refers to values as "independent phenomena, which are appreciated by human beings. Beauty, freedom, fairness, dignity, knowledge, friendship, control, privacy, environmental sustainability, etc., are examples of human values" (IEEE, 2021). Another, very broad definition of values can be found in the literature on Value Sensitive Design, which defines values as "what a person or a group of people consider important in life" (Friedman et al., 1996, p. 349). This definition is difficult to distinguish from mere preferences, as values are, by definition, things that people consider important and valuable though not all things considered important are necessarily values.

Of course, we do not only speak of moral values. There are also aesthetic values, which reflect our appreciation of beauty and artistic expression, as well as the economic value of innovations, which is often measured in terms of efficiency, profitability, and market impact. However, moral values carry a stronger normative weight, as they are deeply intertwined with our sense of obligation, responsibility, and justice, guiding us not just in what we prefer but in what we ought to do.

5.3 Challenges of the Values Approach

Although the turn toward values provides accessibility and a shared vocabulary, it also brings significant conceptual and practical challenges. The flexibility of the concept of value comes at a cost. If we do not clearly define what we mean by values, we risk using the term in an inconsistent or even superficial way. Are we referring to guiding principles, desirable outcomes, or inherent properties of technology? We can term this issue the *contested nature of values* that leads to ambiguity. Without clarity, discussions about values in software engineering may remain vague, making it difficult to implement ethical considerations in a meaningful and systematic way. This means when we aim to build an AI system that is fair, we are left with the question: *What definition of fairness?* It has been famously noted that there are multiple, sometimes incompatible definitions of fairness (Pfeiffer et al., 2023). For example, an algorithm could satisfy one notion of fairness (equal false-positive rates across groups) while violating another (equal outcomes across groups). Verma and Rubin (2018) provide an overview and "explain why the same case can be considered fair according to some definitions and unfair according to others" (ibid.) This contested nature is not limited to fairness. Values like privacy can mean data confidentiality or control over information or freedom from surveillance, depending on context. The list goes on and on. This suggests that the apparent ease of using values to communicate what we consider important may be imprecise. Once we begin discussing tangible implementation strategies, we must return to philosophical reflection and acknowledge the need for domain-specific definitions and concepts (Chap. 4). This does not mean that the *value-centric* vocabulary is useless; it simply reminds us that every remedy comes with its own side effects. The language of values is largely agnostic with regard to the various theories of normative ethics, which is an advantage in terms of acceptance but a disadvantage in terms of practicality for specific action guidelines. Therefore, they can only serve as the starting point for normative considerations by helping locate ethical opportunities and shortcomings. Thus, it could be argued that invoking values can become rhetorical if we do not specify clearly what we mean. Vague commitments to *values* might sound good but lack substance. Consequently, a challenge is to define and operationalize values with precision, and often this requires making hard choices between competing interpretations.

The problem is not that values like fairness or privacy lack ethical weight but rather that they are under-defined and under-contextualized due to their general nature. We can call this the underdetermination of values. Values need to be broad so that they may encompass many situations, yet this decreases practicability. Moreover, there is no algorithm—or meta-principle—to decide which value should be prioritized in a given case. And without a clear hierarchy or method of resolution, developers may face what feels like a free-for-all: they cherry-pick the values most convenient, use values to justify the design path already taken (ex post justification), or fall back on gut feeling and intuition (Gogoll et al., 2021).

Ironically, this process strips the notion of values of its initial simplicity and may return us to square one. This challenge may be called the difficulty of operationalization or the challenge of value implementation. Using the concept of values or not, the underlying problem remains the same: moving from abstract values to concrete technical requirements is an inherently difficult task. There is often a gap between high-level principles and the day-to-day implementation decisions during the development process that some call the *principle-practice gap*. Operationalizing values into software systems involves the translation of values into something more accessible and concrete in order for them to be implemented and at the end measured. This is a process that is far from straightforward or simple but rather a challenging task built on the human ability of ethical deliberation and judgment as well as expertise in software development. The main reason is that some values simply do not easily translate into quantifiable metrics, i.e., requirements: think, for instance, about justice or human dignity. Others might require new design techniques or even mathematical or technological breakthroughs to achieve their implementation (e.g., achieving both privacy and explainability at the same time might demand novel cryptographic or AI methods). However, value-led design can sometimes be achieved without requiring advanced technological skills, for instance, by minimizing data collection or choosing not to develop certain features. Additionally, typical software engineering practices historically have not included (ethical) value checks. Requirements typically focus on functionality, performance, or cost with ethics considered if at all only ad hoc. Changing this requires new methods. As we will see below, some values, the ones that have their origin in the technology itself, may lend themselves easier to empirical testing than others. There is work being done on tools like bias detection toolkits, model explanation techniques, or data governance frameworks, which may very well provide more practical applicability, yet those approaches are still evolving.

5.4 Values Provide Orientation: Values as an Epistemic Tool

To avoid arbitrariness and ethics whitewashing, it is essential to understand how to accurately identify and justify values, making them more accessible and actionable within software engineering processes (Zuber, 2022). This is also the moment where we begin to identify what is actually at stake ethically, formulating a *case for ethics*. Seen from a high vantage point, ethical deliberation breaks down into three broad stages: (1) identifying values, (2) deliberating on how to address and weigh values, and (3) implementing solutions into the artifact (operationalization).

While ethical discussions in software engineering often focus on the second and third steps—balancing competing values or translating them into technical requirements—the first step is frequently overlooked. Yet it is here that values prove especially powerful: as an *epistemic tool* (or a tool for ethical insight), values offer a productive lens through which we can analyze the ethical landscape of a concrete software artifact (Zuber et al., 2024).

Rather than serving immediately as normative imperatives, values can be used heuristically to *spot* ethically significant features of a system or development project. When viewed this way, the common critiques of values such as their contested nature, their context-dependence, or their difficulty of operationalization are far less concerning. At the epistemic stage, we are not yet committed to resolving value conflicts or embedding specific value trade-offs in code or system design. Instead, values help us *highlight potential areas of ethical relevance* and focus our analysis. They guide our attention toward challenges and opportunities that might otherwise be overlooked, offering a structured way to make the ethically relevant visible. Here we are not too much concerned with methods for allocating or assigning risks; instead, we focus on identifying relevant values and determining how to prioritize them.

By treating values as an epistemic entry point, we can begin to map out the ethical terrain of the software we are developing. This mapping lays the foundation for the next phases of deliberation and implementation, ensuring that ethical analysis is grounded in the specificities of the artifact and its environment, rather than in abstract theory alone.

As outlined in Chap. 2, our discussion of digital technology identified three key perspectives that must be considered when thinking about software. Each of these perspectives carries significant implications for the normative evaluation of software systems:

1. Software as a Means to an End: Some software systems function primarily as tools, helping users achieve specific goals or tasks. In this role, they are judged based on their effectiveness, efficiency, and alignment with user intentions.
2. Software as an Interpreter of the World: Software often acts as a filter, interpreting or presenting aspects of the world to its users without their full awareness or control. This interpretive power shapes user experiences and influences how reality is perceived, raising important ethical considerations about transparency and user autonomy.
3. Software as a Shaper of Social Norms: Software can also shape behavioral expectations, defining what is considered normal or acceptable within specific social contexts. By doing so, it can influence social domains and the boundaries between them, creating new forms of interaction and potentially redefining social norms.

These three perspectives offer explanations of digital transformation: in some way, the deployment of a digital device can alter the individual's relationship to the world and to others. Therefore, it is crucial to focus on those moments in which the deep structure of the (human-)human-world relation is transformed (Ihde, 1990). Such transformations deserve particular attention if we aim to evaluate technology from an ethical standpoint.

However, these perspectives alone are not sufficient for a thorough ethical analysis since often ethical opportunities are rooted in the unique technical features of software systems. These technical features often define the spaces where values are embedded, expressed, and perpetuated. Hence, they act as critical interfaces making them hinges for ethical evaluation.

Those key technical features include (c.f. Chap. 2):

- Data Dependency: Software increasingly relies on vast amounts of data for decision-making and personalization, raising concerns about privacy, bias, and data governance.
- Scalability: Software systems can scale rapidly, potentially amplifying both positive and negative impacts across large populations.
- Malleability: Software is highly adaptable, allowing for rapid changes but also making it challenging to ensure consistent ethical standards.
- The Imperceptible Nature of Software: Software often operates in the background, making its influence on user behavior and decision-making less apparent.
- Integration with the Human Mind: Many software systems interact directly with human cognitive processes, influencing perception, memory, and decision-making.
- Persuasive Computing and the Ethical Challenge of Influence: Some software is explicitly designed to shape user behavior, raising questions about manipulation and user autonomy.
- Social Power of Software: Software can reinforce or disrupt power dynamics within societies, affecting everything from social interactions to political participation.

- Diffusion of Responsibility: The collaborative nature of software development can obscure accountability, making it difficult to assign responsibility for negative outcomes.

Taken together, these perspectives that stem from technical characteristics not only shape how software systems function but also influence how they are perceived, utilized, and held accountable. This makes them essential elements in the broader discussion of software ethics, as they define the contexts in which values are embedded, expressed, and potentially challenged. We will explore this in more detail in Chap. 6.

When we use values as an epistemic tool to identify potential chances and challenges, another distinction seems plausible: values that are inherent to the technology and values that can be found in the (social) context or domain in which the artifact will be deployed. Understanding these two categories of values allows us to systematically navigate ethical complexity. We will now explore this in more detail.

5.5 Two Kinds of Values: Techno-Generic and Domain-Specific

When developing ethical software, we need to consider not just *what* a technology does but also *where* and *how* it will be used. This means recognizing two key areas where values come into play: the values that emerge from the technology itself and the values that are shaped by the social domain in which the technology operates.

We can think of these as two complementary perspectives:

1. **Techno-generic values**: Values that arise from the nature of the technology, regardless of where it is used
2. **Domain-specific values**: Values that are tied to the context or sector in which the software is deployed, such as healthcare, education, or law

This distinction allows us to better understand and anticipate the ethical challenges of software development. Some concerns are embedded in the digital artifacts themselves. Think of data privacy in machine learning or explainability in AI. Others emerge only when we examine how these tools interact with human practices, institutions, and expectations, like fairness in hiring algorithms or autonomy in medical decision support systems. Furthermore, we can now better understand where different types of solutions can be found: techno-generic approaches can be addressed by concepts such as AI Ethics, Big Data Ethics, Computer Ethics, and Professional Ethics, whereas domain-specific challenges need to incorporate domain-specific ethics into the analysis (see Chap. 4).

Techno-generic values thus can be seen as *ethics from the inside out*. The idea of techno-generic values refers to the ethical concerns that are built into, or strongly associated with, specific technologies. These are values that any responsible development team should take into account from the start regardless of the domain. They emerge from the technology itself and are thus always to be considered if a given technology is used. These values are therefore legitimate because they stem from the very nature of the technology itself, particularly from the unique features that distinguish software systems ethically from tools like a hammer (c.f. Chap. 2). For example, machine learning systems routinely raise questions of fairness, bias, transparency, data privacy, and robustness. These values are not domain specific; they stem from the technical features and limitations of the tools themselves. Similarly, autonomous systems—like self-driving cars or automated decision-making algorithms—raise issues of accountability and control, regardless of where they are applied. Essentially, all of these unique features serve as critical touchpoints where values are disclosed and acted upon, making them essential considerations for ethical software development. They shape the contexts in which values like privacy, fairness, transparency, and accountability are expressed and validated.

Domain-specific values, on the other hand, can thus be understood as ethics *from the outside in*. They reflect the norms, principles, and expectations of the field or the domain in which the software will be used. We need to understand that in order to build ethically sound software, we need to understand not just the technology but also the people, professions, and societal systems. Every domain has its own value structure and its own idiosyncratic normative demands. For instance, in healthcare, the core value is healing. In education, values such as student agency may take precedence. In law enforcement, the stakes might revolve around proportionality, due process, and transparency. Importantly, the same technology can have very different ethical implications depending on the domain. A facial recognition tool used to unlock a smartphone carries less ethical challenges than one used by police to identify suspects. In the first case, a mistaken match may be an inconvenience. Yet it still constitutes discrimination if an entire group of people is denied access due to technological limitations. In the second, it could mean wrongful arrest or worse. To navigate this, we can draw on the field of domain ethics, which seeks to highlight the normative demands specific to each domain.

So why does that distinction matter for our purpose of spotting ethical issues? Recognizing the difference between techno-generic and domain-specific values helps development teams and management make better ethical decisions. It enables them to ask more precise questions at each stage of the process:

- What values are inherent in the technology we are building? → techno-generic! → Ethics of technology, i.e., Ethics of AI, Big Data Ethics, etc.
- What values are crucial in the environment where this software will be used? → domain specific! → Domain Ethics, i.e., Bioethics, Medical Ethics, Educational Ethics, Environmental Ethics, etc.

It also reminds us that ethical software development is not one size fits all but depends heavily on the concrete software artifact and its domain of application. A technically fair algorithm might still violate the norms of a particular professional context. And a tool designed with privacy in mind might still undermine trust if it fails to respect deeper cultural or institutional values.

Good normative software design requires both perspectives: Techno-generic values place the spotlight on the system to ensure it is technically sound and fair. Domain-specific values highlight the context it will be used in to ensure it allows for morally good actions in the world.

5.6 Values in Conflict

Even when values are identified and agreed upon, real-world design often demands balancing them against each other. This is the problem of trade-offs between values. It is common that pursuing one value can *impinge* on another. Figure 5.1 illustrates a graphical representation of possible trade-offs. For instance, there is a well-known tension between privacy and security: increasing one can reduce the other (e.g., encrypting data promotes privacy but may make oversight for security harder, whereas extensive surveillance might boost security at the cost of privacy). The EU's Trustworthy AI report (2019) explicitly acknowledges that "[i]n situations where the implementation of the key ethical requirements creates conflicts between them, decisions on the trade-off (i.e. the decision to choose to fulfil one ethical requirement over another) should be evaluated continuously." Accuracy vs. fairness is a classic conflict in the world of artificial intelligence: the most accurate

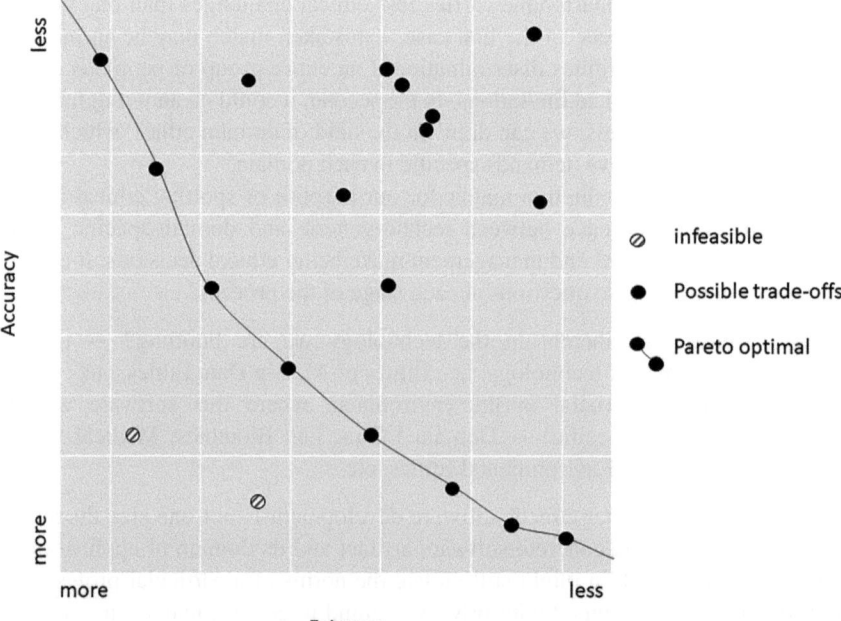

Fig. 5.1 Trade-off between accuracy and fairness and Pareto optimality

prediction model might be one that inadvertently discriminates, so ensuring fairness might require sacrificing some accuracy or adding constraints. These conflicts mean that designers often have to prioritize or find *trade-off strategies*. This is difficult and sometimes controversial: whose values win out? For example, should an AI prioritize fairness over performance if the fairest outcome slightly reduces overall accuracy? Different stakeholders might answer differently. The key critique here is that value-based design isn't as simple as ticking off a list of all good things—it requires ethical deliberation about how to balance values when they clash. Failing to acknowledge trade-offs can lead to systems that inadvertently undermine one value while chasing another. So while the software system remains in the upper-right portion of the graph, it is possible to improve the situation by increasing adherence to either value—or even both—thereby moving closer to the respective axis (i.e., toward the origin). Once the product reaches the line, however, boosting compliance with one value (however you would measure it) necessarily diminishes compliance with the other. This line marks the Pareto optimality, or efficiency frontier, since everything after the line is simply infeasible, the trade-offs on the line are pareto efficient. Although it is generally uncontested that software should be designed to efficiently optimize the chosen values, it is far from evident which position on that line—i.e., which Pareto-optimal trade-off—ought to be realized (Gogoll et al., 2021) as some favor one value over the other and vice versa.

Furthermore, in software development, values are often framed in terms of risks: bias is the risk of discrimination, while a lack of transparency poses risks to adoption and fairness. The ethics of risk, then, requires us to ask: What criteria should we use to assess whether a risk is morally legitimate? Is mere acceptance sufficient, or must we also consider a duty of care? In either way, ethical values must first be examined to determine the nature of the risks that arise when they are violated. To achieve ethical software development, the first challenge is ensuring that knowledge about ethical values is accessible to both management and the development team (see Chap. 6). In the literature on ethical software development as well as in other non-academic publications, different approaches to value setlist in software engineering have emerged: The first major task is to identify and articulate values.

Since we are concerned not with interests but with values, we must learn how to identify, justify, and apply them in a structured and non-arbitrary way. To guide this process, we adopt a triadic model that links each methodological step with its specific aim. We will briefly introduce the three phases and then take a deeper look at the first two: value identification and justification. The third phase, implementation, is addressed through established approaches such as Value Sensitive Design (Friedman, 1996; Friedman et al., 2013) and Value-Based Engineering (Spiekermann & Winkler, 2022; Spiekermann, 2024).

5.7 The Ethically Informed Triad: From Normative Analysis to the Technical Implementation of Value-Oriented Information Systems

We follow a triadic model that is structured in three main phases, which can be understood both vertically as sequential stages and horizontally as an iterative cycle. Its goal is to systematically, reflectively, and justly integrate values into digital technological design processes.

Phase I: Identifying Ethically Relevant Aspects (Chap. 6)
  This initial phase corresponds to the conceptual exploration of the context. It focuses on uncovering normatively significant aspects by analyzing both the specific domain (domain value analysis) and the characteristics of the digital technology itself, applying the techno-generic ethical concepts introduced in Chap. 2. At its core, this phase involves a philosophically grounded inquiry into relevant values and a systematic stakeholder analysis. The goal is to elucidate the structure and significance of key values and to identify both direct and indirect stakeholders who may be impacted by the technology.
Phase II: Deliberation and Prioritization of Ethically Relevant Aspects (Chap. 7)
  This second phase forms the deliberative core of the design process. It involves evaluating and prioritizing the previously identified values, goal conflicts, and potential courses of action through participatory negotiation. While conventional approaches often lack robust methodological guidance for this step, the incorporation of discourse ethics offers a procedural framework for normative reasoning and the resolution of value conflicts.
Phase III: Embedding Ethically Appropriate Solutions into the Software Artifact (Chap. 8)
  The third phase focuses on translating the results of ethical deliberation into concrete technological implementations. This includes both the prospective design of new systems and the retrospective evaluation of existing technologies. Approaches such as *Ethics by Design*, *Value-Based Engineering*, and *Value Sensitive Design* exemplify this phase. The emphasis lies in specifying and implementing both functional and non-functional requirements in ways that embody the identified values within the system's architecture and behavior.

In this book, however, we argue for the additional necessity of embedding these ethical reflections—developed in Phases I and II (Chaps. 6 and 7)—within an overarching organizational framework (Chap. 8). While the operational details of software development methods and relevant technical standards are crucial for this integration, they fall beyond the scope of this volume and would require a dedicated second volume.

The triadic model represents an integrative, iterative, and normatively grounded design framework. By connecting ethical analysis, deliberative legitimization, and technical implementation, it enables the structured development of value-sensitive and human-centered technologies. This approach responds to central criticisms of

VSD, particularly its lack of formalized decision-making procedures and offers a model for systematically addressing value conflicts in technology design.

References

Aristotle. (2014). In R. Crisp (Ed.), *Aristotle: Nicomachean ethics*. Cambridge University Press. (Original Work published 350 B.C.).

Friedman, B. (1996). Value-sensitive design. *Interactions, 3*(6), 16–23.

Friedman, B., Kahn, P. H., Jr., Borning, A., & Huldtgren, A. (2013). Value sensitive design and information systems. In N. Doorn, D. Schuurbiers, I. van de Poel, & M. Gorman (Eds.), *Early engagement and new technologies: Opening up the laboratory* (pp. 55–95). Springer.

Gogoll, J., Zuber, N., Kacianka, S., Greger, T., Pretschner, A., & Nida-Rümelin, J. (2021). Ethics in the software development process: From codes of conduct to ethical deliberation. *Philosophy and Technology, 34*(4), 1085–1108.

High-Level Expert Group on Artificial Intelligence. (2019). *Ethics guidelines for trustworthy AI*, 6. Retrieved July 18, 2025, from https://digital-strategy.ec.europa.eu/en/library/ethics-guidelines-trustworthy-ai

IEEE. (2021). *IEEE 7000-2021 standard model process for addressing ethical concerns during system design* (pp. 1–82). IEEE. https://doi.org/10.1109/IEEESTD.2021.9536679

Ihde, D. (1990). *Technology and the lifeworld: From garden to earth* (Vol. 560). Indiana University Press.

Jobin, A., Ienca, M., & Vayena, E. (2019). The global landscape of AI ethics guidelines. *Nature Machine Intelligence, 1*(9), 389–399.

Kant, I. (2017). *Kant: The metaphysics of morals*. (M. Gregor, Trans., L. Denis, Ed.). Cambridge University Press. (Original work published 1797).

Mill, J. S. (1863). *Utilitarianism*. Parker, son, and Bourn. Retrieved from the Library of Congress, https://www.loc.gov/item/11015966/

Nyholm, S. (2022). *This is technology ethics: An introduction*. John Wiley & Sons.

Pfeiffer, J., Gutschow, J., Haas, C., Möslein, F., Maspfuhl, O., Borgers, F., & Alpsancar, S. (2023). Algorithmic fairness in AI: An interdisciplinary view. *Business & Information Systems Engineering, 65*(2), 209–222.

Shilton, K. (2018). Values and ethics in human-computer interaction. *Foundations and Trends in Human–Computer Interaction, 12*(2), 107–171.

Spiekermann, S. (2024). The 10 principles of value-based engineering. In *Corporate digital responsibility* (pp. 33–58). Nomos Verlagsgesellschaft mbH.

Spiekermann, S., & Winkler, T. (2022). Value-based engineering with IEEE 7000. *IEEE Technology and Society Magazine, 41*(3), 71–80.

UNESCO. (2021). *Recommendation on the ethics of artificial intelligence*. Retrieved from https://bsu.buap.mx/b2m

Van de Poel, I. (2021). Design for value change. *Ethics and Information Technology, 23*(1), 27–31.

Verma, S., & Rubin, J. (2018). Fairness definitions explained. In *Proceedings of the International Workshop on Software Fairness* (pp. 1–7).

Zuber, N. M. C. (2022). *Ethik in der Softwareentwicklung*. Doctoral dissertation, lmu.

Zuber, N., Gogoll, J., Kacianka, S., Nida-Rümelin, J., & Pretschner, A. (2024). Value-sensitive software design: Ethical deliberation in agile development processes. In H. Werthner, C. Ghezzi, J. Kramer, J. Nida-Rümelin, B. Nuseibeh, E. Prem, & A. Stanger (Eds.), *Introduction to digital humanism: A textbook* (p. 637). Springer Nature.

Open Access This chapter is licensed under the terms of the Creative Commons Attribution 4.0 International License (http://creativecommons.org/licenses/by/4.0/), which permits use, sharing, adaptation, distribution and reproduction in any medium or format, as long as you give appropriate credit to the original author(s) and the source, provide a link to the Creative Commons license and indicate if changes were made.

The images or other third party material in this chapter are included in the chapter's Creative Commons license, unless indicated otherwise in a credit line to the material. If material is not included in the chapter's Creative Commons license and your intended use is not permitted by statutory regulation or exceeds the permitted use, you will need to obtain permission directly from the copyright holder.

Chapter 6
Spotting the Right: Overcoming Moral Uncertainty

"We see only what we know"
"Man sieht nur, was man weiß"

Johann Wolfgang von Goethe, letter to Friedrich von Müller

Abstract Ethical software development begins not with decisions but with perception: recognizing when and where ethical questions arise. This chapter addresses the foundational phase of ethical practice—hence spotting the right—and examines the epistemic challenge of identifying morally significant aspects in software design. This chapter argues that ethical problems in digital technologies often go unnoticed not because they are absent but because the conceptual tools to recognize them are lacking. To overcome this moral ignorance or uncertainty, software producers must learn to detect both techno-generic and domain-specific values, develop ethical sensitivity, and shift their perspective from seeing software as merely neutral tools to recognizing them as transformative artifacts. Using the example of avalanche safety apps, the chapter outlines a structured approach to context analysis, stakeholder inclusion, and value identification, demonstrating how ethical awareness can be integrated into early design phases. It emphasizes that ethical reflection is not a separate or burdensome activity but a practical, interdisciplinary method that enhances decision-making, fosters shared responsibility, and aligns technical development with human values. This phase is essential for ensuring that what is ethically relevant becomes visible—and only what is seen can be addressed.

Having achieved conceptual clarity regarding the nature and role of values, as well as the conditions under which ethical theories apply, we have also identified the characteristics of digital technologies that render them morally significant in their own right. This insight reveals that software systems demand more than merely user-focused ethical assessments. With this foundation established, we are now equipped to pinpoint the case for ethics.

The quote at the top serves a purpose for this chapter—*We see only what we know* (Goethe, 1949). Goethe's insight reminds us that perception is often limited by understanding—an idea that also holds true in software development. If we lack the conceptual knowledge to recognize ethical values, we simply may not see them. Yet, to design ethically sound software, we must learn to look beyond our default perspectives or things that merely happen to be on our radar at that moment. Behavioral scientists call this pull toward whatever is top-of-mind availability bias: when a theme dominates public discussion—e.g., dataset bias in AI—it crowds out attention to quieter but equally important issues. Because the salient problem monopolizes the spotlight, other ethical dimensions risk being ignored. We need to train ourselves to spot where technologies intersect with values, human rights, or moral norms because only what is seen can be properly addressed.

In the world of software development, ethical problems often remain invisible during the development process, not because they do not exist but because no one has been trained to spot them and methods that might help are not implemented. A feature is shipped, a dataset is cleaned, and a user interface is streamlined. Everything seems to work until someone asks: Should we be doing it like this? Did we not think about that?

Unlike some mechanical or technical failures, ethical issues do not saliently raise alarms or necessarily crash programs. They may hide in the background: in biased data, exclusionary defaults, opaque algorithms, or user decisions quietly shaped by automation. Before we can make good ethical decisions, we must learn to recognize when ethics is even at stake. This is harder than it sounds. It requires a shift in perception from seeing software as just a tool to seeing it as a social and moral force (Chap. 2). This chapter is about deepening that ethical sensitivity, not to overload developers with more responsibilities but to empower them with a new lens. Ethics, here, should not be a burden but a mode of understanding, a way of seeing more clearly what software actually does in the world.

Software engineers often feel they lack the responsibility or authority to address ethical concerns, seeing themselves merely as tool builders (Chap. 2). Others may acknowledge their responsibility but are unsure where to begin, what ethical issues to look for, and, once identified, how to make informed decisions. This is completely understandable; after all, these demands add to the already-complex and practical task of coding software (Alpsancar, 2023). We will show how ethics can serve as a practical guide for software developers and why ethical reasoning is not something to fear or even worse reserved for experts in ethics only.

Furthermore, we will stress the concept of deliberative ethics, which stresses the need for collective moral reasoning among team members (Chap. 3), fostering shared responsibility and dialogical decision-making within development contexts. This might be enacted through structured team workshops where developers, designers, and domain experts collaboratively explore ethical demands such as which values are normatively demanded or how to balance personalization with user privacy and autonomy to justify their decisions.

Hence, let us frame our endeavor as building moral strength, fostering clarity, resilience, and alignment with ethical principles in our decisions and actions. Building this moral strength involves two key components: identification and decision-making.

1. First, it requires recognizing the relevant ethical aspects of a situation—what we can call the identification challenge. Often, moral issues are not immediately apparent, particularly in fields like information technology, such as software development. This involves ensuring that there is indeed a case for ethics, which philosophers might refer to as the *epistemic* aspect of moral uncertainty. Recall that we covered major ethical theories and concepts relevant to case-based ethical evaluation.
2. Second, once moral questions or value conflicts are identified, the challenge shifts to making reasonable decisions. This means weighing competing reasons and ultimately arriving at a course of action, a task we can call the decision challenge. Even when we recognize the relevant factors, we may struggle with prioritizing or balancing values or normative demands against one another.

   (a) It is also important to briefly consider the phenomenon of *akrasia*, or weakness of the will, since not every good or well-reasoned decision necessarily leads to corresponding action. This disconnect highlights a central challenge for any account of practical reasoning and ethical agency. Although *akrasia* plays a critical role in understanding why even virtuous agents may fail to act accordingly, the following chapters will not explore this theme in detail. Its omission is deliberate, as the focus remains on the cultivation and contextualization of *power of judgment and decisiveness* as a virtue, rather than on internal failures of volition.

While answering these questions, we make sure that the situation present represents a case for ethics.

6.1 When Does a Question Stop Being Technical and Start Being Ethical? A Case for Ethics?

In everyday life, normativity is institutionalized through laws and regulations, cultural norms, and social expectations, defining what is acceptable or unacceptable behavior. Laws, for instance, set boundaries by declaring certain actions illegal, often aligning with moral standards to prevent harm or injustice. Actions that are punishable are frequently also morally reprehensible because they violate shared ethical values, such as fairness, respect, or responsibility. Fraud, such as deliberately deceiving someone for financial gain, is both illegal and morally unacceptable. In fact, at least in free and democratic societies, laws and ethics should usually enjoy a high correlation. Laws prohibit fraud to protect individuals and organizations from economic harm and to maintain fairness in transactions. Fraud violates ethical principles of honesty, trust, and justice. It exploits others' vulnerabilities for personal benefit, which most moral theories deem wrong. However, moral evaluations may sometimes go beyond legal boundaries. For instance, while exaggerating qualifications on a job application may hardly ever lead to legal consequences, it is still considered ethically questionable because it undermines trust and fairness. Yet not all illegal actions are inherently immoral. For example, whistleblowing might violate confidentiality laws but can be ethically justified when it exposes corruption or protects public welfare. Laws can sometimes enshrine unjust practices or fail to align with evolving moral values. For instance, discriminatory laws based on race, gender, or other biases have been challenged on ethical grounds. Ethics serves as the foundation for questioning and reforming laws that conflict with principles like equality, freedom, and human dignity. Historical movements against slavery, apartheid, or unjust labor laws relied on ethical arguments to advocate for change. Interestingly, many would argue that these practices had always been wrong and that the law is only catching up.

Contrary to formal laws, social conventions are informal rules that govern behavior in society, such as norms around politeness, dress codes, or public conduct. While these conventions promote order and predictability, they are not always aligned with ethical principles, and sometimes breaking them is necessary to address deeper moral issues. Consider the Rapid and Blitz Chess Championships in New York City in 2024 after a dispute over the tournament's dress code. Magnus Carlsen, World No. 1, attended the event wearing jeans, which violated the International Chess Federation's (FIDE) regulations designed to "ensure professionalism and fairness for all participants." Despite being fined $200 and given the opportunity to change clothes, Carlsen declined, leading to his exclusion from round nine and his subsequent withdrawal from the tournament. This incident highlights the tension between social conventions and ethical considerations. While FIDE's dress code represents a social convention aimed at maintaining a certain standard of professionalism, Carlsen's refusal to comply raises ethical questions about individual expression and the relevance of such norms in modern chess. Carlsen's stance suggests a belief that performance and skill should take precedence over adherence to traditional attire, challenging the necessity and fairness of the imposed dress code. Certainly, a measure of desire for recognition and attention as well as personal animosities may have influenced Carlsen's behavior, but the central point still holds. The situation underscores how established conventions can come into conflict with evolving perspectives on personal freedom and authenticity, prompting a reevaluation of which norms serve the best interests of the community and the individuals within it.

Hence, ethics plays a crucial role in evaluating both laws and social conventions. When laws are broken, ethics helps determine whether the action is morally justifiable or if the law itself is unjust and needs reform. While laws provide a framework for acceptable behavior, ethics critiques their alignment with deeper moral principles. Social conventions, though promoting harmony, can sometimes perpetuate outdated or unjust practices. Ethical considerations ensure that both laws and norms reflect moral values. Ultimately, ethics acts as a guide to balance societal expectations with moral responsibilities.

The emergence of new technologies can give rise to entirely new domains of human activity, where established moral values have yet to scrutinize practices and provide corresponding guidance. In these areas, social norms and legal frameworks are still absent. In such cases, ethics plays a crucial role in navigating these uncharted territories, providing guidance in the absence of established laws or societal norms. When a novel technology emerges, it often raises unique and complex moral questions that were previously inconceivable, requiring ethical deliberation to establish principles and practices that align with ethical standards. A compelling example of this is in vitro fertilization (IVF). Before the development of assisted reproductive technologies, conception outside the human body was impossible, meaning that questions regarding the moral status of surplus embryos, parental rights in cases of egg or sperm donation, and the ethical implications of genetic screening were simply not relevant. The advent of IVF forced society to confront these new ethical realms, leading to evolving perspectives on reproductive rights, medical intervention in fertility, and the responsibilities of parents, doctors, and lawmakers in shaping reproductive policies.

Whenever we encounter such situations, we must scrutinize them ethically. For example, facial recognition technology is widely used for security and surveillance. While it may be legal in many jurisdictions, ethical concerns arise regarding its potential misuse, such as its impact on vulnerable communities. Scrutinizing its use requires asking *ought-to* questions: Should this technology be deployed without transparency? Ought it prioritize privacy over efficiency? By ethically analyzing its implications, we ensure its application aligns or even fosters with ethical values or principles. Hence, we can identify a case for ethical evaluation.

This awareness is also critical in delineating ethical responsibility: it allows organizations and teams to understand who is accountable for specific moral questions, whether they emerge during requirement engineering, algorithm design, deployment, or post-release monitoring. Without this sensitivity, ethical responsibility may be neglected or deflected often in favor of minimal legal compliance or profit-driven considerations. Therefore, integrating ethical thinking into software development is not merely an added layer of compliance. It is a foundational aspect of responsible engineering. It opens the door to systematic reflection on how values are embedded in technologies, how trade-offs are negotiated, and how societal impacts are considered. It provides the basis for establishing a culture in which ethical awareness becomes part of professional identity and daily decision-making, ensuring that software systems are not only functional and lawful but also aligned with broader human and societal values.

6.2 Epistemia: Knowing What to Look at and What to Look for

In summary, ethics plays a crucial role by addressing gaps that laws and institutional rules often leave open. While rights can offer clear boundaries, they typically cover only the most extreme cases, leaving many everyday situations unresolved. Even when laws are well defined, depending solely on courts to enforce them is impractical due to the high transaction costs involved, if everyone pushed actions to the legal limits, the sheer volume of the resulting litigation would be both overwhelming and prohibitively expensive. Conventions, on the other hand, might be outdated or culturally biased, failing to adapt to evolving contexts. Interests can be grounded in self-interest, lacking broader ethical consideration, while values might seem arbitrary or insufficiently justified. Ethics bridges these gaps by systematizing principles and critically evaluating actions, decisions, and their broader implications. This is clearly a case for considering ethics in both its positive and negative dimensions: as a guiding force that orients our actions toward desirable or valuable principles (which is always the case when new technologies emerge) such as recognizing a value and actively seeking to foster it. Alternatively, ethical reasoning helps navigate value conflicts and balance competing interests. In this context, ethics involves making trade-offs, and failing to engage with these conflicts means overlooking their moral significance (Chap. 7).

But how can ethics be effectively integrated into software development? Do we need to hire experts who guide us through the process? And who is actually required to understand the ethical challenges that arise in the context of software engineering? We need technological expertise but also a clear understanding of which outcomes are desirable and which circumstances might be morally problematic. Importantly, we need to talk about what is desirable, so that the process becomes a discourse grounded in information.

6.3 Who Needs to Be Part of the Ethical Discourse?

The integration of ethical deliberation into technology development represents a procedural approach that goes beyond isolated ethical assessments, enabling ongoing reflection throughout the process (Chap. 8). In order for deliberation to serve as an effective instrument for ethical reflection and decision-making, it requires a systematic understanding of its structural foundations. A structured deliberation process begins with contextualization: it is essential to clarify which domain or area of application is involved and what kind of expert knowledge is needed both in terms of the technology itself and its domain, most often a societal subsystems, in which it is deployed. Here, the empirical sciences, applied or domain ethics, and technology ethics play a central role. In addition, corporate values, codes of conduct (CoCs), and publicly available mission statements must be taken into account as important normative reference points. Legal expertise also contributes a crucial perspective, particularly regarding regulatory compliance. Lastly, stakeholder and user inquiries are vital to identify needs, interests, acceptance, and potential value conflicts at an early stage. Only on the basis of such a broad, interdisciplinary, and participatory foundation can deliberation be effectively anchored as a systematic practice within development processes. When taken seriously, deliberation enables the integration of both top-down and bottom-up approaches. In this process, we identify values, laws, and conventions; principles that must be respected and aligned with throughout software development. By combining these normative demands with stakeholder interviews and legal expertise, we can address both dimensions effectively. The initial phase of deliberation—epistemic reflection—requires a thorough exploration of context.

6.4 Designing for the Mountains: Ethical Development of Avalanche Safety Apps

Let us consider an example to illustrate how one might initiate and navigate an ethical deliberation process. It is important to recognize that ethical software development can be conceptualized as a structured procedure comprising three core phases: (1) identifying ethically relevant aspects, (2) deciding how to prioritize ethically important aspects of the project, and (3) embedding ethically appropriate solutions into the software artifact (Zuber et al., 2020). This framing gives rise to a critical question: where should such an analysis begin, especially given the dynamic and reciprocal interplay between technology, users, and society? Equally important is the question of participation: who must be involved in this process? Ethical deliberation is not the sole responsibility of ethicists or developers alone. Rather, it demands the inclusion of diverse perspectives from domain experts, designers, and legal advisors to end users and affected stakeholders. Only through such inclusive participation can ethically relevant concerns be adequately surfaced, contested, and integrated into design decisions.

Avalanche risk assessment tools offer a concrete case for exploring this question. These systems mediate critical decisions in high-risk environments, blending probabilistic data analysis with on-site assessment. To identify the key ethical questions in their design and deployment, we must ask how such technologies shape responsibility, trust, and decision-making under uncertainty. This includes distinguishing between issues that require interdisciplinary expertise, such as snow science or behavioral psychology, and those that are fundamentally normative, such as the appropriate balance between human judgment and algorithmic guidance, or the ethical implications of shifting blame in the event of an accident. We must also consider how to navigate competing moral claims: which ethical demands such as the duty to inform, protect, or empower users warrant action and how they should be operationalized in technical design and user communication. Addressing these questions calls for a systematic approach to ethical analysis that can identify when ethical reflection is essential.

We designate this stage of examining the context and purpose of the software system as context exploration. This phase involves collecting facts and contextual information relevant to the scenario (Bleisch et al., 2021). The contextual description therefore serves as a crucial foundation for ethical evaluation and the identification of morally relevant aspects. We can emphasize this as part of the identification challenge or *spotting the right phase* and understand it as a process that is inherently linked to specific roles and areas of expertise. We will proceed step by step, exploring different domains, clarifying whom we need to consult, and determining the types of questions we ought to ask (Zuber et al., 2020, 2022b, 2024). At first glance, the development of an avalanche safety app for ski tours may not seem to raise complex ethical issues, as its goal is simply to enhance safety for ski tours, a valuable goal as such. But the end does not justify the means. To ethically assess avalanche safety apps, it is essential to involve a diverse range of experts and stakeholders. Each group contributes critical knowledge and normative perspectives necessary to ensure that ethical reflection is both grounded and comprehensive. Specifically, the following actors are needed (Table 6.1):

Together, this interdisciplinary and participatory approach enables that ethical considerations are not only reactive or compliance based but proactively integrated into the very foundation of design, development, and deployment (Fig. 6.1). An ethical deliberation process that involves only a subset of these components risks overlooking critical dimensions of harm, bias, or exclusion. Each group of context experts, corporate actors, legal advisors, stakeholders, and ethicists contributes uniquely to shaping a technology that is not just functional but aligned with ethical values. In the high-stakes context of avalanche safety, this multidisciplinary collaboration is not optional: it is a condition of responsible design.

Now let's look at who's responsible for bringing the right knowledge into the process so the team can make a solid moral judgment. Before any decision can be made, the team first needs to gather the facts. To make this clearer, we'll walk through an example showing who needs to bring what kind of knowledge when we're working on our avalanche safety app.

6.4.1 Domain Knowledge

The first step is to gather expert knowledge about the factors that contribute to avalanches, focusing on two key areas: Either we focus on the indoor phase or on the outdoor endeavor. In the indoor phase of avalanche risk assessment, typically conducted at home during tour planning, decisions are based on two key categories of parameters: snow conditions and terrain characteristics. Central to the snow-related assessment are the danger level and core zone information provided in the avalanche bulletin, which indicate regional hazard levels and particularly affected elevations and slope aspects. Modern methods like the Quantitative Reduction Method (QRM) (see Schmudlach, 2021; Munter, 2017) combine these inputs into a continuous Danger Indicator (DI), using interpolation and transition zones to reflect more nuanced risk levels. On the terrain side, slope angle is the most critical factor, but advanced systems also account for additional features such as slope size, curvature, terrain breaks, and vegetation, as reflected in a Terrain Indicator (TI). Tools like Skitourenguru integrate these quantitative parameters with digital elevation models and route data to evaluate risk along planned tours. Together, these snow and terrain

6.4 Designing for the Mountains: Ethical Development of Avalanche Safety Apps

Table 6.1 Areas of expertise for the informed identification of ethically relevant aspects

Needed areas of expertise for informed identification of ethically relevant aspect	Role	Expert
1. **Domain knowledge**	Understanding of the application domain, including its key concepts, structures, and needs	Context experts: Experts in geology, snow science, and alpine safety are vital for defining the application's scope and grounding ethical reflection in real-world use contexts. They offer domain-specific insights into environmental patterns, behavioral risks, and how alpine terrain interacts with human decision-making. Their knowledge ensures that ethical inquiry is not abstract but situated within the lived realities of mountain sports
2. **Technology expert**	Technical expertise regarding architectures, frameworks, infrastructure, and development practices	Engineers, software developers, and systems designers bring knowledge of how digital flaws and unintended consequences can arise. They are essential for identifying technical vulnerabilities and designing safeguards or fail-safes
3. **Rights and standards**	Knowledge of legal frameworks, industry standards, norms, and compliance requirements	Legal experts: Legal scholars and data protection officers ensure that ethical deliberation operates within regulatory frameworks. They define what is legally permissible, clarify liability structures, and highlight obligations related to data governance, privacy, and risk communication
4. **Domain ethics**	Ethical considerations inherent to the specific domain, focusing on normative implications and social impact	Ethicists: Beyond assessing what is acceptable or accepted, ethicists are responsible for identifying omissions, values, or risks that may be ignored or underrepresented. Their role is not merely to evaluate after the fact but to participate in shaping the design process from the outset with a focus on anticipatory responsibility
4. (a) **Ethical theories as value identification method**	Use of ethical theories (e.g., deontology, utilitarianism) to identify and articulate values	

(continued)

Table 6.1 (continued)

Needed areas of expertise for informed identification of ethically relevant aspect	Role	Expert
4. (b) **Corporate values and CoCs**	Offers normative orientation based on organizational principles	Company representatives: Organizational guidelines provide a normative compass that shapes internal decision-making. Compliance officers, CSR managers, and ethics advisors contribute to aligning product development with the company's mission, societal commitments, and reputational goals. In moments of ethical tension, such as trade-offs between usability and safety, their perspective becomes especially important for formulating acceptable and justifiable choices within the company's own ethical posture
5. **Stakeholders**	Identification and analysis of all individuals or groups affected by or involved in the system	Users (Skiers): As the primary beneficiaries and operators of the app, skiers provide insights into practical usability, expectations, habits, and potential misuse. Their experiential knowledge is critical for aligning design with real-world needs Regional communities and environmental experts: Since ski touring takes place in ecologically sensitive and often inhabited areas, it is crucial to include local communities and environmental stakeholders. Their perspectives ensure that the technology respects place-based values and contributes to sustainability
6. **Moderators**	Communication needs to systematize moral warrants; this requires skilled moderators	Ethicists interdisciplinary facilitators play a central role in guiding dialogue across diverse domains of knowledge. They help uncover blind spots, question prevailing assumptions, and foster reflective engagement. Their expertise ensures that ethical deliberation remains balanced, inclusive, and attentive to both immediate usability and long-term societal impact

parameters form the foundation of probabilistic planning methods, which aim to exclude high-risk terrain before entering the field.

However, algorithms can process large volumes of data to detect patterns that are difficult for humans to recognize. Looking ahead, algorithms are expected to play an even greater role in avalanche risk assessment by offering more precise and personalized evaluations. Nevertheless, they cannot replace the need for classic, on-site assessments by experienced ski tourers, which remain essential for safe decision-making in complex terrain.

6.4 Designing for the Mountains: Ethical Development of Avalanche Safety Apps

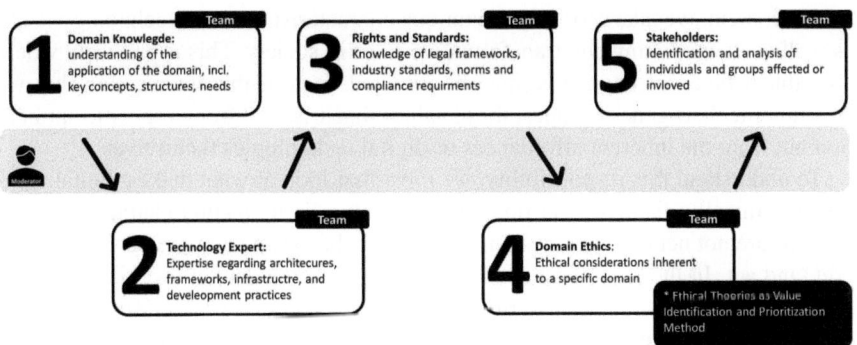

Fig. 6.1 Spotting the Right—a structured approach

On-site behavior in the field, particularly in relation to avalanche danger, involves a continuous process of observation, evaluation, and decision-making that cannot be replaced by prior planning alone. It is typically divided into the on-site evaluation and the individual slope assessment. On-site newly available information such as current weather, snow conditions, track frequency, and warning signs must be used to verify and, if necessary, revise the initial tour plan. The evaluation of the individual slope demands detailed, slope-specific analysis involving both expertise and structured methods: assessing the slope angle and aspect, micro-terrain, and potential avalanche problems and conducting stability tests like the small block test, often supported by tools like the LARA app. Risk assessment also includes evaluating the potential consequences of a slide and accounting for human factors and group dynamics. Standard safety measures, such as maintaining spacing in steep terrain, are essential and must be adapted based on slope characteristics and danger level. Throughout, the regional avalanche bulletin serves as a reference but must be critically interpreted on-site. Effective risk management in the field requires the integration of planned information with real-time observations, ongoing reflection, and adaptive decision-making to minimize avalanche danger on individual slopes.

6.4.2 Technology Expert

Digital technologies are no longer passive instruments: we interact with them, rely on them, and increasingly delegate parts of our thinking and decision-making to them. Nowhere is this more evident than in high-risk environments, where tools like avalanche safety apps promise not only convenience but potentially lifesaving guidance. Yet with that promise comes a particular set of ethical challenges. These challenges stem not only from the context of use in the backcountry, under uncertain conditions, among diverse user groups, but also from the very nature of digital technology itself. For software engineers, this presents both a responsibility and an opportunity: to shape technologies that are not only effective but ethically informed.

In this context, we take seriously the unique characteristics of the technology itself, as well as its mediating and transformative roles in society. This is precisely where the ethical focus of engineers must be directed. It is at this intersection that we encounter techno-generic values, those values that arise not from a specific application but from the inherent affordances of digital technologies themselves.

To understand this responsibility, we must first look at what makes digital technology ethically distinct. One fundamental feature is its medial character: digital systems are not neutral windows onto the world; they shape how we perceive, interpret, and act. In the case of an avalanche app, the way a danger level is visualized through color codes, icons, or warning phrases can profoundly affect a user's behavior (Table 6.2). Developers, in collaboration with designers, should reflect on these effects. Seemingly small choices in interface design may escalate or downplay perceived risk. Here, ethical responsibility begins with an awareness that perception is always mediated and that mediation is a design choice.

A second defining feature is the dynamic and emergent nature of digital systems (Table 6.2). Unlike physical safety equipment, a digital app is never truly finished. Its models may be retrained, its features updated, and its interfaces refined. But with each change, consistency may suffer. What if a user receives different risk assessments for the same conditions due to a model update? Trust can erode when users are left in the dark. Software engineers can mitigate this by introducing version transparency, in-app changelogs, or update notifications that explain what has changed and why. Ethical design, in this sense, involves more than correctness; it involves continuity and communication.

Digital systems are also defined by their networked and ubiquitous nature. Connectivity enables real-time data, sharing of locations, or live updates from authorities. But it also introduces ethical tension, particularly around surveillance and autonomy. A feature that enables GPS tracking may enhance safety, yet at the cost of privacy or the cherished solitude of alpine touring. Additionally, constant tracking may drain the battery especially in cold weather, which could pose a safety risk down the line. Engineers can navigate this by building in strong privacy controls such as opt-in features, anonymous modes, or local data storage and by foregrounding user consent. Ethical design does not mean avoiding powerful features but offering users meaningful control over them.

The malleability of digital technology adds another layer. Avalanche safety apps are not static tools. They are shaped by the intentions, assumptions, and values of their makers. Engineers are uniquely positioned to decide which users an app is for: should it default to beginner-friendly recommendations or support expert-level customization? By designing for configurability, perhaps offering both simple and advanced modes, engineers acknowledge the diversity of users and resist a one-size-fits-all approach. The ethical dimension here lies in recognizing design as a normative act: every feature is an expression of priorities.

Relatedly, digital tools occupy a position of power. As users grow accustomed to relying on apps, those tools begin to carry silent authority. A danger level displayed in red is rarely questioned. This is particularly troubling when users override their own training or instincts in deference to the app. Engineers can address this by

6.4 Designing for the Mountains: Ethical Development of Avalanche Safety Apps

Table 6.2 Identifying ethical implications, values, and implementation strategies

Aspect	Ethical implication	Values	Suggested actions
Medial character	Design shapes perception and behavior	Interface choices influence perceived risk	**Reflect on UI choices:** • Regularly user-test visual cues and warnings • Provide clear explanations alongside color or icon indicators • Offer contextual tooltips to avoid misinterpretation
Dynamic nature	Frequent updates may confuse users	Ensure transparency	**Inform about changes:** • Clearly document updates (changelogs) • Notify users explicitly about major model changes • Allow users to compare previous and updated assessments
Networked ubiquity	Surveillance and autonomy conflicts	Balance utility and privacy	**Enable privacy:** • Use opt-in settings for tracking features • Enable local data storage and anonymization • Clearly communicate privacy trade-offs to users
Malleability	Design encodes values and assumptions	Autonomy: cater to diverse user needs	**Give users autonomy:** Provide multiple user modes (beginner/expert) • Allow configuration of risk thresholds or detail level • Transparently document assumptions behind recommendations
Authority and influence	Apps may override user judgment	Foster user reflection and autonomy	• Embed second opinion reflective prompts ("Check current conditions onsite") • Encourage double checking data through external sources • Clarify limitations of automated recommendations
Persuasiveness	Design may subtly manipulate users	Nudge toward informed, reflective decisions	• Make default options explicit and justifiable • Design UI to enhance informed decision-making • Regularly evaluate the software for unintended influence

(continued)

Table 6.2 (continued)

Aspect	Ethical implication	Values	Suggested actions
Diffuse responsibility	Hard to locate accountability	Increase traceability	• Make data sources and model limitations visible • Provide clear attribution of decision recommendations • Include visible disclaimers highlighting user responsibility
Algorithmic opacity	Users must trust black-box outputs	Promote algorithmic transparency	• Prefer interpretable models or provide explanation layers • Include breakdowns of contributing risk factors • Allow users to explore the "why" behind recommendations interactively
Scalability and impact	Small choices scale unpredictably	Anticipate consequences at scale	• Conduct simulations to anticipate unintended large-scale outcomes • Monitor user patterns to identify environmental impact • Regularly revisit and adapt recommendations based on emerging data
Datafication and quantification	May marginalize non-quantifiable knowledge	Participation: integrate qualitative insights	• Integrate qualitative inputs from local experts • Allow users to annotate and share observations • Complement quantitative scores with local narratives and advice

embedding moments of reflection into the interface, e.g., reminders to check conditions on-site, links to full avalanche reports, or prompts that encourage second opinions. At a more subtle level, digital technologies influence behavior. Whether through default options, interface design, or persuasive elements, users are nudged often without noticing. A suggested tour or a simplified "safe" label may encourage certain decisions while discouraging others. Engineers, in this context, become behavioral architects. Their ethical responsibility lies in ensuring that nudges support informed, reflective choices rather than manipulating users toward convenience or risk-taking. Technology should assist judgment, not replace it.

Yet with increased reliance comes the risk of diffused responsibility. When something goes wrong, responsibility may be unclear. Was it the developer's fault for providing flawed data? The user's, for misinterpreting it? Or is the fault located somewhere in the complex network of systems and decisions? Engineers cannot resolve this entirely, but they can build systems that make decision paths traceable and limitations visible. Rather than hide behind legal disclaimers, apps can openly communicate what they know, how they know it, and where uncertainty lies. Here we need to think about accountability.

6.4 Designing for the Mountains: Ethical Development of Avalanche Safety Apps

This brings us to the opacity of algorithms, one of the most urgent ethical issues in contemporary tech. If an app generates a high risk label, but the logic behind it remains hidden in a machine learning model, users are left to either trust blindly or ignore the result. Developers can respond by prioritizing explainability through visual breakdowns of contributing factors, hoverable tooltips, or even interpretable models over black-box systems. Ethical engineering, in this sense, means making systems legible and trustworthy.

The scalability and reach of digital tools further heighten the ethical stakes. A design decision that seems minor in testing can have widespread effects once the app is in broad use. For example, a "recommended route" feature might inadvertently concentrate users on certain trails, increasing pressure on fragile ecosystems or overburdening rescue services. Here, engineers can simulate behavior at scale, model unintended consequences, or design adaptive systems that respond to usage patterns and ecological concerns. Ethical foresight becomes part of the development process.

Finally, digital technology operates through datafication and quantification: it transforms environments, experiences, and judgments into data points. Avalanche risk becomes a number, a color, and a graph. While this allows for precision and prediction, it also risks marginalizing forms of knowledge that do not fit into data structures such as local intuition, embodied experience, or community memory. Engineers can counteract this by building in space for qualitative input, letting users annotate conditions, contribute observations, or consult local expertise alongside algorithmic predictions. This highlights user participation.

Taken together, these ten aspects show that digital technology is not just a means to an end. It is a shaping force. When we design for the mountains, we do not simply build apps; we participate in reshaping how risk is perceived, how knowledge is structured, and how decisions are made. For software engineers, this is not a reason to retreat from complexity but a call to act with care, creativity, and humility. Ethical reflection need not stand apart from engineering practice. It can and should be part of how we write code, structure interfaces, and imagine the tools we put into the world.

In the context of avalanche safety, this means more than avoiding harm. It means honoring the values of autonomy, responsibility, and respect for nature that have long defined alpine culture. It means designing technologies that amplify judgment rather than replace it. And it means recognizing that, in the end, every line of code written for the mountains carries with it an ethical trace.

6.4.3 Rights and Standards

In addition to gathering domain knowledge, it is essential to examine the legal aspects surrounding avalanche safety and ski touring. This includes understanding regulations, responsibilities, and standards at local, national, and international levels. Relevant topics to explore are liability in case of accidents, the legal obligations of ski tourers and guides, and protected areas where ski touring might be restricted. Descriptive questions to guide this exploration include: *What are the legal responsibilities of ski tourers and rescue services in avalanche zones?* or *Which laws govern ski touring in protected alpine regions?* Incorporating these legal insights ensures the app provides not only safety guidance but also aligns with relevant laws. It is crucial to recognize that legal rights are deontological: They are absolute in nature, and only rights can be weighed against other rights. Preferences, cultural norms, or subjective opinions, for example, cannot outweigh fundamental rights such as freedom of expression or privacy.

While the legal implications of avalanche accidents involving the use of digital tools and apps are not explicitly addressed in the sources, several relevant aspects can be inferred. Most importantly, personal responsibility remains central: even when using decision-support tools like Skitourenguru (based on the QRM) or LARA, users are not absolved from their duty to make independent, on-site judgments. These apps are framed as recommendations, not legal standards, and their use does not carry direct legal consequences unless broader laws or duties of care are violated. Of course, one can imagine legal regulations being introduced that prohibit these apps from even suggesting routes through areas deemed too dangerous. In the case of LARA, user competence and training may be relevant in legal evaluations, particularly regarding negligence. There is also concern about cognitive biases, such as anchoring effects from app-based risk maps, which may lead users to neglect critical slope-specific assessment. Although no specific legal rulings or regulations are cited, general principles of due diligence, personal accountability, and negligence would likely apply. In the event of an accident, the user's behavior, knowledge, decision-making process, and the context in which the app was used would all be subject to legal scrutiny. The use of an app might be one factor among many but would not in itself constitute a breach of duty unless it replaced essential, situational judgment inappropriately.

These are normative questions. But these questions are addressed by legal experts and compliance officers.

6.4.4 Domain Ethics

Social conventions play a crucial role in managing alpine regions, especially in areas where no formal laws regulate certain behaviors, such as giving wild animals the right of way. Instead, established behavioral guidelines help prevent accidents and minimize disturbances caused by ski tourers. To promote safety and environmental responsibility, international skiing organizations have introduced codes of conduct that, while not legally binding, serve as essential guidelines.

Unlike codified legal regulations, social conventions in alpine environments emerge through community practices and expert recommendations, e.g., Deutscher Alpenverein (DAV) (Deutscher Alpenverein, 2025). These conventions mitigate risks related to avalanche safety, wildlife preservation, and the prevention of accidents on ski slopes. These behaviors, though not legally mandated, are essential for maintaining a sustainable and safe mountain environment.

Information relevant to this domain can be found in local municipal regulations, in guidelines from umbrella organizations like ski or alpine associations, and in areas of applied ethics such as environmental or animal ethics. These sources contain values and norms that guide respectful and responsible interaction with nature, along with rules on how to uphold them. We refer to these as domain-specific values since they arise from the specific context of mountain sports and environmental stewardship, not from the digital technology itself. Their relevance stems from the cultural, ecological, and institutional setting in which the technology is used.

Nonetheless, these values should be taken into account when developing an avalanche safety app, because they shape the expectations, responsibilities, and behaviors of the people using the app. Ignoring them could lead to solutions that are technically sound but culturally or ethically misaligned. Integrating domain-specific values ensures that the app supports not just safety but also respectful engagement with the natural environment and existing community practices.

For example, applications can provide real-time behavioral feedback, alerting users when their actions deviate from established safety and environmental norms. By leveraging GPS tracking and algorithmic recommendations, digital nudging enhances awareness and accountability, encouraging compliance with best practices. However, challenges remain regarding overreliance on automated guidance and the balance between guidance and enforcement. While such technologies can improve safety and environmental stewardship, their effectiveness depends on transparent implementation that complements, rather than replaces, traditional

Table 6.3 Identifying domain-specific values, responsibilities, and implementation strategies

Aspect	Domain-specific values	Design responsibility	Suggested actions
Social conventions	Environmental responsibility; respectful skiing	Respect and reinforce established community norms	Incorporate codes of conduct, enable normative feedback mechanisms
Environmental ethics	Sustainable attitude	Recognize local norms and environmental ethics	Embed contextual awareness and relevant guidelines in app design; provide education, alerts, and reflective nudges
Ethics of responsibility	Restraint, humility, and foresight	Balance nudging with user autonomy	Use transparent prompts, avoid over-enforcement
Risk ethics	Caution, respect, and attentiveness; modesty	Promote responsible behavior under uncertainty; users should acknowledge limits and uncertainty	Design for precaution, context-sensitivity, and awareness; include features that caution users, reflect risk realistically
Liberal ethics	Autonomy: Freedom must be exercised responsibly	Enable responsible self-determination	Respect user choices while ensuring no harm to others or environment

community norms and personal judgment. Future research should examine the long-term behavioral effects of digital interventions and their ethical implications in outdoor recreation.

Normative concerns arise in different forms here (Table 6.3). First, we must identify which conventions and attitudes are considered desirable and assess whether they still align with our convictions so that we can actively foster them. Second, we need to recognize when these desirable norms might be violated by implementation of our digital tools and determine how to address such conflicts. Both of these aspects are fundamentally moral questions and must be taken seriously.

At this intersection, risk ethics becomes especially relevant. It prompts us to ask how we should act under uncertainty and what responsibilities we bear when our actions carry potential harm to other humans or non-humans. At the same time, digital ethics asks similar questions in technologically mediated contexts: How can we behave responsibly within specific social subsystems, especially when power and knowledge are unequally distributed? Both ethical fields emphasize the need for context-sensitive, precautionary, and relational approaches where value-oriented reflection guides action without defaulting to restriction alone. This allows for the cultivation of moral responsibility.

Following and actively promoting values that provide orientation and help sustain social subsystems is essential: Truthfulness is a core value that ensures the functionality of the social subsystem of communication. If people systematically lie and no one can assume that what is being said is true, trust breaks down in personal interactions as well as in public discourse. Understanding becomes impossible, as communication relies on the basic expectation that statements are at least intended to be truthful. Without this orientation, language turns into a tool of manipulation rather than a medium for shared meaning. This shows that without actively promoting and adhering to fundamental values like truthfulness, communication loses its stabilizing role in society.

Similarly, in the context of human-nature relations, the example of ski touring in the mountains illustrates the importance of values that foster a respectful and sustainable attitude toward the environment. Such behavior is not merely a question of personal preference or lifestyle but a reflection of social and ecological responsibility. Drawing on environmental philosophy, particularly Aldo Leopold's *ethics of environment* (Leopold, 1989), this perspective is grounded in a relational ethic that sees humans as integral members of an ecological community. If we fail to act in ways that respect the integrity and balance of this community, we undermine the very systems that sustain life. Promoting values such as respect, care, and ecological responsibility is thus essential to maintaining a positive and constructive relationship with nature. This also entails the value of modesty: A recognition of the limits of human control and the unpredictability of natural systems. As Hans Jonas (1979) emphasized in his *ethics of responsibility*, acting under conditions of uncertainty, especially in high-risk environments, demands restraint, humility, and foresight. In the case of mountain sports, this translates into taking responsibility for one's physical and mental capabilities and making decisions that reflect self-awareness rather

6.4 Designing for the Mountains: Ethical Development of Avalanche Safety Apps 95

than overconfidence. Modesty, then, becomes a stabilizing value, one that enables both safety and sustainability by fostering caution, respect, and attentiveness.

One might conclude that, to minimize ecological and personal risk and uphold responsibility, the best course of action would be to abstain from ski touring altogether or even to legally forbid it. However, this introduces a tension between autonomy and caution and invites reflection on proportionality: Is it morally justified to prohibit an activity entirely, or can responsible engagement be guided by regulation, education, and a value-conscious attitude?

When considered together, the values derived from both the technological characteristics and the specific domain context support a principalist approach, one that emphasizes the deliberate integration and promotion of these values in the design of an avalanche safety app. Importantly, the combination of both perspectives not only strengthens ethical reflection but also helps identify potential omissions: values or norms that might be overlooked if one perspective is considered in isolation (Zuber et al., 2022a). However, to complete the ethical analysis, we must now turn our attention to the relevant stakeholders and their interests. Understanding their positions, responsibilities, and potential tensions will allow for a more comprehensive and context-sensitive ethical framework.

Table 6.4 Applying ethical theories to the ski touring app case study

Ethical theory	Focus	Guiding questions (with examples)
Deontology	Duties, obligations, and rules	Are there aspects of the system that violate moral or professional duties? For example, *a ski tour app sharing or even using GPS data without consent* Does the system encourage neglect of obligations? For example, *an algorithm that allows ski tourers to bypass sustainable mountaineering practices* Would we want everyone to act this way? For example, *automating decision-making without appeal mechanisms*
Consequentialism	Outcomes and consequences	Who benefits, and who might be harmed? For example, *a ski tour navigation app that improves ski tour traffic for some while displacing it to locals* Are the benefits fairly distributed? For example, *an avalanche monitoring feature that is only available on premium devices*
Virtue ethics	Character, moral agency, and virtues	What virtues or vices does the system encourage? For example, *a gamified ski tour app that promotes dangerous behavior* Are the developers acting with integrity and care? For example, *a team refusing to release a biased model* Does the system foster empathy or responsibility in users? For example, *a ski tour app that encourages mountain and safety education by enhancing collaboration instead of competition*

6.4.5 Ethical Theories as Value Identification Method

Ethical theories support the identification of ethically relevant cases by guiding us through their characteristic modes of questioning and critical reflection (see Chap. 4; Table 6.4).

6.4.6 Stakeholders

Discussions on ethical software development often recommend holding stakeholder workshops—or at least inviting stakeholders to share their values and concerns—and with good reason. Spotting ethical issues requires viewing a problem from multiple perspectives and imagining how others might be affected. Stakeholders, broadly, are anyone touched by your product or decision. Stakeholders are often categorized as direct or indirect, legitimate or illegitimate, or according to their power to influence the development process. In this chapter, we remain at a general level, since determining which stakeholders are relevant depends on the specific context. For our avalanche app example, we will present a selection of stakeholders that we consider appropriate for illustrative purposes. Involving them reduces blind spots that even well-intentioned teams inevitably have. In many cases, stakeholders not only offer helpful perspectives but may also have a legitimate—sometimes even moral—right to be heard. This is particularly true when software directly affects individuals' autonomy or privacy, such as workplace tools that analyze employees' emails or messages using sentiment analysis. Admittedly, some stakeholders may pursue their own political or commercial goals, but gathering their viewpoints and arguments is still invaluable: it surfaces hidden risks, reveals overlooked values, and yields a more balanced picture than any purely "armchair" analysis could provide.

When identifying stakeholders for an avalanche safety app, we must consider all individuals, groups, and entities that influence or are influenced by avalanche safety in ski touring. Primary stakeholders include ski tourers, mountain guides, and rescue services, as they are directly impacted by risks and the app's functionality. Ski tourers often prioritize freedom of movement and personal responsibility over strict safety protocols, valuing their autonomy in decision-making. In contrast, mountain guides depend on reliable and precise information, as they carry the responsibility for the safety of their entire group. Meanwhile, rescue services may advocate for features like mandatory GPS tracking to improve emergency response times and increase the chances of successful rescues. These differing priorities highlight the ethical challenge of balancing autonomy, responsibility, and safety when designing an avalanche safety app. Addressing these tensions requires thoughtful compromises that respect the needs and values of each stakeholder group.

Secondary stakeholders encompass tourism boards, local authorities, and insurance companies who have a vested interest in promoting safe practices and managing liabilities. Tertiary stakeholders involve environmental organizations advocating for habitat protection, foresters, residents, and data providers like weather stations ensuring compliance with regulations and rights. Key questions include: *Who benefits directly from safety measures? Who bears responsibility for risk management?* and *What conflicts might arise between stakeholders, such as conservation or environmental efforts* versus *tourism needs?*

Consulting stakeholders primarily involves gathering their interests, needs, and concerns to ensure their perspectives are incorporated into decision-making. This process helps identify what each stakeholder values most, such as safety, accessibility, environmental protection, or profitability. For example, ski tourers may prioritize accurate real-time avalanche warnings, while rescue services may focus on efficient emergency response systems. Tourism boards might emphasize promoting safe and sustainable tourism, whereas environmental organizations may advocate for minimizing disruption to wildlife and ecosystems. Even animals, considered indirect stakeholders, represent ecological interests that should be accounted for when planning routes and activities.

Key questions for gathering interests include: *What does each stakeholder aim to achieve? What are their primary concerns or risks?* and *Where might stakeholder interests align or conflict?* By understanding and balancing these interests, the app can address diverse priorities and foster collaborative, sustainable solutions.

Balancing conflicting interests is an inherently ethical task. Weighing options, prioritizing values, and making a justified decision are a moral endeavor. A case for ethics arises whenever interests are in conflict, and there is uncertainty about the right course of action.

6.5 Avalanche Apps as a Case for Ethics

We introduced the concept of techno-generic values, meaning that digital technology itself brings about specific ethical considerations that need to be addressed regardless of the particular context in which it's used. These are values that emerge from the nature of digital tools: for example, privacy, transparency, autonomy, explainability, or trust.

In the case of our avalanche safety app, this means that ethical reflection is not just about content or user needs, it is also about how the technology operates. For instance, if the app uses algorithmic risk assessments, we need to consider how understandable those assessments are to users (explainability), whether users feel free to make their own decisions (autonomy), and whether they trust the app's suggestions (trustworthiness). These values are not optional add-ons; they are part of what responsible technology development requires from the start.

Adding domain-specific values is equally important, and these often stem from established conventions or a historical awareness of practices within the field. In avalanche risk assessment, for example, values like self-responsibility, local knowledge, and community trust have long played a central role. These values are shaped by the history of alpine sports and the cultural practices of mountain communities.

Ignoring them in favor of purely technical solutions could lead to a mismatch between the app and the real-world contexts in which it is used. By acknowledging and integrating these domain-specific values, developers can create technology that aligns more closely with the expectations and responsibilities of its users supporting not only safety but also a respectful continuation of long-standing traditions. Further domain-specific values can also be identified by taking a look at domain ethics, in our case environment ethics, animal ethics, or sport ethics. Especially when we recall that avalanche decision-making typically involves two distinct phases (planning and on-site deliberation), it becomes clear why both techno-generic and domain-specific values must be considered. In the planning phase, users gather and interpret information, often using digital tools like our app. In the on-site phase, however, decision-making relies more heavily on personal experience, training, and situational judgment. This is where domain-specific values such as autonomy, self-responsibility, and embodied knowledge become especially relevant.

When developing an avalanche safety app for ski tours, we have seen that ethical concerns can arise, also because conflicts with existing ski conventions can lead to further ethical concerns. For instance, in some regions, there are long-standing local practices where ski tourers rely on community knowledge or informal guidelines rather than official forecasts or digital tools. Introducing an app that standardizes risk assessment might unintentionally undermine this local expertise or shift responsibility away from personal judgment toward the app's recommendations. This raises ethical questions about respecting local practices, responsibility in decision-making, and the potential overreliance on technology. If users begin to trust the app more than their own observations or community advice, it could lead to risky behavior in situations where the technology falls short. Developers need to consider how to integrate with, rather than override, these conventions perhaps by including local insights or allowing space for user input, so that the app supports, rather than replaces, responsible and context-sensitive decision-making.

Additionally, different stakeholder interests may diverge and require compromises through trade-offs. For example, experienced backcountry skiers might want detailed, expert-level risk data to make their own informed decisions. In contrast, less experienced users might prefer simplified warnings or clear recommendations, like "Do not proceed." Designing the app to cater to both groups involves a trade-off: presenting too much technical detail could overwhelm novice users and lead to poor decisions, while oversimplifying risk levels might frustrate experts or even encourage risky behavior by giving a false sense of security. Balancing these needs ethically means thinking carefully about how risk information is presented, how user autonomy is respected, and what the app's responsibility is in shaping behavior on the mountain.

Digital technologies like avalanche safety apps raise ethical issues not only due to their technological nature but in how they function socially. Techno-generic values such as explainability, autonomy, and trust emerge from the nature of digital tools and must be considered from the outset. At the same time, domain-specific values—like self-responsibility, local knowledge, and community trust—are rooted in the traditions of alpine sports and play a vital role in on-site decision-making.

Ethical concerns arise when technology disrupts these established practices, for example, by shifting responsibility away from personal judgment or marginalizing local expertise. Additionally, designing for different user groups—experts vs. novices—requires careful ethical trade-offs in how risk is communicated. These are not just questions of usability or design: they are ethical challenges at the heart of responsible technology development.

References

Alpsancar, S. (2023). What is AI ethics? Ethics as means of self-regulation and the need for critical reflection. *International Conference on Computer Ethics, 1*(1).

Bleisch, B., Huppenbauer, M., & Baumberger, C. (2021). *Ethische Entscheidungsfindung: Ein Handbuch für die Praxis*. Versus Verlag.

Deutscher Alpenverein München & Oberland. (2025). *Skitouren—Die Königsdisziplin im Winter*. Retrieved July 24, 2025, from https://www.alpenverein-muenchen-oberland.de/alpinprogramm/winter/skibergsteigen

Goethe, J. W. (1949). *Gedenkausgabe der Werke, Briefe und Gespräche*. Stuttgart, Artemis-Verlag, 1949–1962, 1.

Jonas, H. (1979). *Das Prinzip Verantwortung: Versuch einer Ethik für die technologische Zivilisation*. Suhrkamp Verlag.

Leopold, A. (1989). *A Sand County almanac, and sketches here and there*. Oxford University Press.

Munter, W. (2017). *3×3 Lawinen: Risikomanagement im Wintersport*. Athesia Tappeiner Verlag.

Schmudlach, G. (2021). Avalanche risk property dataset (ARPD). *Skitourenguru*. Retrieved from https://info.skitourenguru.ch/index.php/data/212-arpd

Zuber, N., Kacianka, S., Nida-Rümelin, J., & Pretschner, A. (2020). Ethical deliberation for Agile software processes: EDAP manual. In M. Hengstschläger & the Austrian Council for Research and Technology Development (Eds.), *Digital transformation and ethics* (pp. 150–177) Ecowin Verlag.

Zuber, N., Gogoll, J., Kacianka, S., Pretschner, A., & Nida-Rümelin, J. (2022a). Empowered and embedded: Ethics and agile processes. *Humanities and Social Sciences Communications, 9*(1), 1–13.

Zuber, N., Kacianka, S., & Gogoll, J. (2022b). Big data ethics, machine ethics or information ethics? Navigating the maze of applied ethics in IT. *arXiv preprint arXiv:2203.13494*.

Zuber, N., Gogoll, J., Kacianka, S., Nida-Rümelin, J., & Pretschner, A. (2024). Value-sensitive software design: Ethical deliberation in agile development processes. In H. Werthner, C. Ghezzi, J. Kramer, J. Nida-Rümelin, B. Nuseibeh, E. Prem, & A. Stanger (Eds.), *Introduction to digital humanism: A textbook* (p. 637). Springer Nature.

Open Access This chapter is licensed under the terms of the Creative Commons Attribution 4.0 International License (http://creativecommons.org/licenses/by/4.0/), which permits use, sharing, adaptation, distribution and reproduction in any medium or format, as long as you give appropriate credit to the original author(s) and the source, provide a link to the Creative Commons license and indicate if changes were made.

The images or other third party material in this chapter are included in the chapter's Creative Commons license, unless indicated otherwise in a credit line to the material. If material is not included in the chapter's Creative Commons license and your intended use is not permitted by statutory regulation or exceeds the permitted use, you will need to obtain permission directly from the copyright holder.

Chapter 7
Deciding for the Good: Overcoming Moral Indecisiveness

> "Immaturity is the inability to use one's understanding without guidance from another. This immaturity is self-imposed when its cause lies not in lack of understanding, but in lack of resolve and courage to use it without guidance from another. Sapere Aude! 'Have courage to use your own understanding!'"
>
> Immanuel Kant, What is Enlightenment?

Abstract This chapter addresses the challenges of ethical decision-making in software development. Building upon the initial identification of moral issues, it highlights the necessity of ethical deliberation to navigate value conflicts such as usability versus explainability and safety versus autonomy. Drawing on philosophical traditions (Kant, Aristotle, Rawls, Habermas, and Toulmin), it emphasizes the importance of autonomy, practical wisdom (phronesis), and reflective equilibrium in making morally sound judgments. The chapter illustrates that ethical choices cannot be resolved through predetermined rules or purely technical solutions; rather, they require continuous engagement with ambiguity and pluralism. Through participatory processes involving diverse stakeholders, developers can systematically clarify, contextualize, and balance conflicting values. Real-world examples, including avalanche safety apps, underscore how context-sensitive reasoning and stakeholder dialogue enrich ethical decisions. Ultimately, the chapter argues for fostering an organizational and professional culture where ethical deliberation is embedded into everyday practice, empowering teams to actively shape technology toward morally desirable outcomes.

If we consider autonomy to be a core value, it is essential that we cultivate the capacity to think and judge for ourselves. This does not imply that deliberation must occur in isolation. On the contrary, autonomous thinking can and should be practiced within collaborative environments, i.e., teams and organizational structures that encourage open expression, including dissent, even when directed at those in higher hierarchical positions or decision-making roles. Of course, autonomy is often constrained by material realities; for instance, economic dependence may limit the ability to leave unsatisfactory employment. Nevertheless, it remains possible and ethically desirable to foster a workplace culture and professional ethos that values critical reflection. Such a culture contributes to human flourishing. This convergence of ethical reflection in organizational and technological contexts underscores the close relationship between business ethics and technology ethics.

The process of integrating ethics into technology development can be understood as a progression from spotting (the right) to judging to implementation. It begins with spotting values, where the key question is: What ethical issues are at stake? This involves methods such as value elicitation, domain analysis, stakeholder interrogation, and, if necessary, the application of ethical theories (Chap. 6). Next is deliberation, which seeks to understand how these values and perspectives relate to the specific artifact being developed. This stage builds upon and deepens the participatory foundations established during the identification phase, relying heavily on workshops, dialogue, and collaborative methods to refine ethical insights and surface practical concerns. The deliberation's central task is to determine which values are relevant and why, using approaches such as balancing, threshold models, stakeholder weighting, and mainly the exercise of practical wisdom. This is what we want to discuss in the following chapter. After that, implementation addresses how these ethical insights are reflected in the design, through attention to technical constraints, the development of requirement specifications, and the establishment of relevant KPIs. The last endeavor draws heavily on technological techniques and methods so we will not discuss it in this introductory book. This stepwise approach ensures that ethical considerations are not just identified but meaningfully embedded in practice.

7.1 Deliberate Decisiveness

Ethical decisions are rarely clear-cut. Just consider the following possible trade-offs within software development: A feature that increases safety may reduce user autonomy. A more explainable algorithm might be less accurate. A bias mitigation strategy could add complexity that makes a system less transparent. These are value conflicts, not engineering bugs. They simply cannot be fully resolved by metrics or compliance checklists. There is also no algorithmic solution where you have a problem as an input and the ethical solution as an output. Instead, they require judgment, either before an algorithm is written or in the interpretation of the output. This became particularly apparent in our discussion of avalanche safety apps in the prior chapter. Tools may prioritize safety through probabilistic planning methods using algorithms, while others may focus on autonomy. Each design choice privileges certain values over others. Thus, raising the question: what is the good we are aiming to support? Or, the question of morality: What qualifies as morally better than the other?

Here lies a paradox: while the turn to values was intended to make ethics more practical and accessible, it does not and cannot eliminate the need for ethical deliberation. On the contrary: It requires and demands it. Values are plural, often vague, and occasionally incommensurable (Chap. 5). This means that deciding for the good involves more than applying a predefined rule or maximizing a single value.

Ethical deliberation is a practice grounded in philosophical reflection and as such a cultivated skill. It may be understood as a form of common sense shaped by experience (pre-theoretical knowledge), as the application of ethical reasoning principles through a conscious cognitive process (e.g. Utilitarianism and Deontology), or as an attitudinal disposition, a kind of character trait, that can be trained and developed across diverse contexts (e.g., Aristotelian Virtue Ethics).

In contrast, ethical theory is a scientific approach to systematize our arguments and actions (Chap. 4). However, in our daily lives, such theories often appear unhelpful. Instead, we rely on the kind of practical knowledge or common sense that comes from lived experience. Aristotle once remarked that no precise rule can tell you why light meat such as chicken is easily digestible; you just learn it by doing it (here: eating it), again and again. Similarly, ethical competence in everyday life is often built not through theoretical abstraction but through practice, reflection, and a feel for the situation at hand. We learn to navigate morally good life not by applying formulas but by developing judgment over time. It is therefore a mistake when "[…] people at large tend to talk as though "ethical principles" or "moral rules" were *exhaustive* of ethics: that is, as though all that moral understanding requires is a commitment to some code of rules which can be accepted as authoritative." (Jonsen & Toulmin, p. 6).

This chapter illuminates what moral judgment in software development actually comprises: how it emerges, how it is practiced, and how it can be cultivated in regard to the digital world. Rather than prescribing a universal rulebook, the aim is to support readers in becoming more aware of their own moral experiences and in developing a reflective stance toward the world. By making this attitude explicit and accessible, the book empowers readers to articulate and deepen the ethical orientation they already exercise in navigating the moral dimensions of everyday life. This reflective capacity is not something entirely foreign to software developers and management or something as if it were reserved for professional ethicists. On the contrary, we are already engaged in moral actions in our daily lives whenever we choose how to treat others, how to weigh responsibilities, or how to respond to perceived injustices. In a way, our normative sensitivity is deeply embedded in our social existence: "We are in effect designed for social life. Our normative capacities are part of the design" (Gibbard, 1990). This means that moral judgment is not an abstract and isolated exercise. Thus, the goal of this book is to rely on our moral reasoning, to help make it visible and deliberate together, especially in the context of designing and working with digital technologies.

7.2 Why Value Ambiguity Is Inevitable

Take the case of the avalanche safety app that we introduced in the previous chapter, which is an avalanche risk assessment tool that generates a traffic-light-style safety rating for entire ski touring routes. One of the key design challenges is how much explanation the system should provide alongside its risk prediction. On the one hand, transparency suggests that users should be informed about how the system arrives at its output: what data were used, how they were weighted, and how the algorithm functions. On the other hand, usability and cognitive load are critical concerns in safety-critical applications. Overwhelming users with complex data or algorithmic logic might decrease the tool's accessibility and effectiveness, especially for non-experts planning their routes under time constraints.

This is where ethical deliberation must enter. Simply because values are underdetermined, they fail to provide specific and concrete guidance. Even worse, they may foster normative indifference, a sense that anything goes, as long as it can be vaguely justified by some value whether taken from a Code of Ethics or found during the epistemic phase. In such cases, ethics is no longer a source of orientation but becomes a rhetorical tool used post hoc. To make ethical reasoning work in practice, we must accept the inevitability of ambiguity and actively engage with it. That means:

- Clarifying and contextualizing values
- Recognizing and mapping trade-offs (see Pareto optimality in Chap. 5)
- Engaging in rational deliberation instead of defaulting to heuristics or gut feeling
- And, most importantly, acknowledging that ethical judgment is not about choosing from a list but about navigating tensions between equally legitimate claims

To provide meaningful and well-founded ethical guidance, the values found in the epistemic or *spotting the right* phase must first be made explicit and interpreted in relation to their context-specific meanings and functional roles. Concrete value conflicts must then be addressed and integrated into a coherent structure capable of guiding action. This process is inherently deliberative. It cannot be successfully navigated through static heuristics or prescriptive rules defined in advance. Ethical principles cannot be straightforwardly translated into case-specific decision-making rules, since values derive their significance from the contexts in which they are applied. Philosophically speaking, software engineers require support to reason through ethical problems casuistically rather than merely applying decontextualized principles (Jonsen & Toulmin, 1988). This is precisely the intention behind the need for a systematic, case-sensitive approach to ethical reflection. Thus, technological artifacts cannot be ethically evaluated from a single perspective; they must be assessed in light of multiple dimensions, including authority, power relations, technical security, feasibility, and prevailing societal values. Consequently, the idea of a ready-made *ethical toolbox* is misleading. Ethical deliberation cannot and should not be fully externalized or delegated.

7.3 Ethical Deliberation in Software Design

We already discussed pluralism in Chap. 4. However, it is most important to stress again and keep in mind that in modern democratic societies, ethical disagreement is not an exception but the norm. As John Rawls famously observed, the very conditions of free institutions and rational deliberation lead to a plurality of reasonable, yet incompatible, moral doctrines. This phenomenon, which Rawls called the "burdens of judgment," notes that while we may reach broad consensus on abstract principles of justice, we are far less likely to agree on specific, applied ethical questions particularly when values conflict. Understood in this way, ambiguity in ethics is not a temporary failure of reasoning but a structural feature of moral life in pluralistic societies. Thomas Nagel (1979) makes a related point: our moral experience is characterized by a fundamental fragmentation of values, meaning that we are guided by multiple, often conflicting, sources of moral concern that cannot be reduced to a single overarching principle. This includes tensions between personal commitments and impersonal duties or between competing values such as loyalty, justice, freedom, and equality. Rather than viewing this as a problem to be solved, Nagel sees this pluralism as an essential feature of ethical life. Moral reasoning involves navigating these tensions, acknowledging that different standpoints (personal, interpersonal, and impartial) can all offer legitimate, yet sometimes incompatible, reasons for action.

In addition to this pluralism of moral perspectives, we must also contend with the general and abstract nature of ethical values and principles themselves. Even when we agree on which values are relevant—such as fairness, autonomy, or safety—their meaning remains incomplete without contextual interpretation. Ethical principles rarely come with built-in instructions for how to apply them in specific, real-world scenarios. As a result, ambiguity arises not only from disagreement between values but also from their inherent openness. They require deliberation, specification, and often difficult prioritization before they can effectively guide action. This central challenge in ethical decision-making in software development stems from what we might call the underdetermination of values (Gogoll et al., 2021). Values are usually presented in abstract, generalized terms. For instance, when we consider codes of ethics, we find that these abstract values are listed without clarification, prioritization, or contextual adaptation. This vagueness gives rise to ambiguity when developers attempt to apply them to specific, real-world situations and concrete software artifacts.

7.4 Deliberative Decision-Making Phase: Navigating Ethical Disagreement

This diagnosis aligns closely with Stephen Toulmin's theory of argumentation, particularly as developed in his book, *The Abuse of Casuistry: A History of Moral Reasoning* (co-authored with Albert Jonsen) (Jonsen & Toulmin, 1988). Toulmin critiques rigid, top-down applications of universal ethical principles and instead revives casuistry, a form of moral reasoning that is case-based, analogical, and context sensitive. Just as Rawls identifies reasonable pluralism as a structural reality, Toulmin offers a method for reasoning through it.

In Toulmin's argumentation model comprising claims, data, warrants, backing, qualifiers, and rebuttals, we find a method for navigating ethical disagreement (Table 7.1). This model acknowledges that moral claims often depend not on formal

Table 7.1 Argumentation models by Toulmin and Jonsen applied to the Ski touring app

Argumentational element	Ski touring: accessibility and sustainability
Claim	Ski touring should remain accessible when paired with digital safety practices
Data	Apps reduce fatalities and improve decision-making in avalanche zones
Warrant	Moral duty to reduce personal and group risk justifies the use of mitigating tools
Backing	Safety guidelines and alpine education emphasize tool-supported responsibility
Qualifier	As long as usage does not foster overconfidence or ecological harm
Rebuttal	Digital tools may encourage broader ecological degradation by expanding access

deduction but on context-specific warrants, which are socially situated and open to contestation. For instance, in debates over environmental responsibility, such as whether ski touring should be restricted to protect mountain ecosystems, different ethical theories produce different but reasonable warrants. These disagreements are not failures of logic but expressions of ethical pluralism grounded in differing value commitments.

This structure reveals how ethical reasoning around emerging technologies is shaped by value-laden assumptions. Here, the warrant hinges on individual responsibility and technological mitigation of risk, which might be compelling from a liberal or utilitarian perspective. But from an environmental ethics perspective, the rebuttal highlights the embeddedness of human action in ecological systems and the limits of technological solutions.

Due to the pluralism or fragmentation of values, large language models (LLMs) often produce outputs that lack consistency in normative domains. They may contradict themselves across tasks, contexts, or time. This inconsistency is a key differentiator from the behavior of rational agents, who strive not merely for logical soundness but for coherence: a sense-making integration of beliefs, values, attitudes, and actions that holds together across contexts. This is possible because agents understand actions not in isolation but as embedded in social contexts. That is, reasoning unfolds within a background of purposes, social meanings, and expectations. A single action makes sense not because it is logically consistent with another but because it coheres within a broader normative pattern (Nida-Rümelin, 2023).

In contrast, usability requires that information be reduced, contextualized, and presented in an intuitive way. Yet this inevitably comes at the cost of losing explanatory detail. This produces an inconsistency between the two values: fulfilling one appears to compromise the other.

7.4.1 A Balancing Game and the Search for Coherence

This tension gives rise to a balancing game of competing priorities: How much explainability can be preserved without undermining usability? How much simplification is acceptable without neglecting ethical responsibility? This is where the idea of coherence becomes relevant, not as formal logical consistency but as ethical and practical integration.

Drawing on John Rawls' concept of reflective equilibrium (Rawls, 1971, p. 49), this means we examine and revise our normative commitments, such as explainability and usability, in light of one another, testing them against our background assumptions until we achieve a balanced, coherent structure. Coherence, then, is not achieved through interest-based compromise but through the deliberative alignment of normative principles embedded in social practices (Nida-Rümelin, 2023).

A coherence-oriented strategy would be to explore how the tension between the two values dissolves when viewed through their social embedding. For example, explainability may not be equally necessary for all users: experienced ski tourers may benefit from detailed risk metrics, whereas less experienced users may need structured action guidance. The app could offer multiple user modes, tailored to social roles and usage contexts such as "expert mode" vs. "beginner mode." In this way, the inconsistency on the level of requirements could be resolved through a coherent embedding in patterns of social interaction.

The apparent incompatibility of explainability and usability does not represent a simple ethical dilemma to be solved by weighing one over the other. Rather, it calls for a deliberative, coherence-seeking negotiation that takes into account social context, cognitive capacities, and normative principles guided by the ideal of reflective equilibrium. In doing so, ethical system design can be oriented toward comprehensibility and trustworthiness, without falling into technocratic reduction or normative overload.

Moreover, Toulmin's emphasis on rebuttals and qualifiers mirrors Rawls's insights about the complexity of judgment. According to Nida-Rümelin (2023), it is essential that ethical arguments must make space for competing views and for the possibility of revising one's stance in light of new evidence or perspectives. Toulmin thus provides a bridge between moral reasoning and democratic deliberation, enabling discourse that respects pluralism while remaining normatively guided. It enables us to reason together about inconsistencies, not to erase differences but to seek coherence across perspectives. Through dialogue, we can uncover shared assumptions, reframe disagreements, and develop practical judgments that are publicly justifiable.

However, such deliberation demands more than voicing preferences or defending fixed interests. It requires that all participants are capable of transcending their immediate interests and preferences, engaging in argument-based reasoning, and accepting that reason, rather than power or assertion, leads the way. Only under these conditions can ethical disagreements become constructive negotiations of reason, rather than polarizing stand-offs.

Hence, ethical deliberation is the process of reasoning together about moral questions. This dialogue can be either with oneself or among a group of people to decide about the priority of values in a certain context. Philosophers characterize deliberation as a method of reaching ethical decisions through discourse, argumentation, and consensus building (Habermas, 1993). It is characterized by the involvement of all participants, recognizing them as valid moral agents obligated to articulate the reasons behind their perspectives and to attentively consider the viewpoints of others (Yetim, 2008, 2011). The primary aim of ethical deliberation is not necessarily to secure unanimous agreement but to enhance understanding through the thoughtful exchange of diverse perspectives.

7.4.2 Judging for the Good

Making a decision is more than selecting among options. It marks the moment when deliberation gives way to action. In uncertain and dynamic environments like the mountains, practical wisdom (*phronesis*) becomes essential. Unlike *sophia*, which seeks timeless truths, or *techne*, which applies fixed techniques, *phronesis* is context sensitive, grounded in experience, and concerned with what truly matters in a given situation. It also differs from mere prudence, which focuses on choosing effective means, without always questioning the value of the ends. Take the example of an avalanche app during a ski tour: while the app might rate a route as low risk based on data, real-world judgment is needed to assess the slope in front of you, factoring in wind shifts, warning signs, group condition, and personal readiness. Practical wisdom involves integrating information from tools without blindly relying on them, recognizing one's limits and prioritizing safety over rigid adherence to plans. In decision theory, the ideal of an optimal solution only applies when a single criterion is at play; real decisions usually involve trade-offs and uncertainty. Thus, decision-making is not just about analysis. It is a dynamic process of structuring problems, weighing values, and acting with integrity and awareness.

The introduction of digital avalanche risk apps can indeed reduce fatalities and make ski touring significantly safer, but this outcome is only achievable if such technologies are developed and used in ways that actively acknowledge and promote key moral values such as truthfulness, modesty, sustainable attitude, and a relational understanding of autonomy. This claim rests on the observation (data) that in both digital communication and outdoor sports, ignoring these values leads to serious breakdowns: in communication, the absence of truthfulness erodes trust and shared understanding, while in mountain environments, a lack of modesty or ecological care can result in personal harm and environmental damage. The underlying warrant is that technologies designed for use in complex, high-risk contexts must not simply function technically but also ethically by reinforcing responsible behavior and thoughtful decision-making. This is supported by backing from ethical theories: Hans Jonas's (1979) imperative to act responsibly in the face of uncertainty, Aldo Leopold's (1970) view of humans as part of an interdependent ecological community, and Onora O'Neill's (2003) understanding of autonomy as something that must be exercised with regard for others and for collective well-being. While the argument holds in most cases (qualifier), some might object (rebuttal) that simply introducing safety technologies should be enough and that emphasizing values adds unnecessary complexity. However, without fostering user awareness, transparency, humility, and respect for environmental limits, such apps may give a false sense of security, be easily misused, or even encourage reckless behavior. Thus, only when digital avalanche apps are guided by and embedded with these values can they truly fulfill their promise of saving lives and supporting a more ethical and sustainable practice of mountain sports.

7.4.3 Software Engineering: Empowerment Through Participation

Clearly, the ability to make decisions and act based on our best reasoning depends on fostering critical thinking; when it is suppressed or discouraged, such reasoning becomes impossible. Hence, it is essential to establish structures that foster and sustain critical thinking or ethical deliberation or moral reasoning rather than marginalize or inhibit it (Zuber et al., 2022). This vision of ethical technology design extends into the practice of methods such as participatory design, where users, stakeholders, and affected communities are actively engaged in shaping technological systems from the earliest stages (Chap. 6). Participatory design moves beyond the traditional model of designing *for* users toward designing *with* them, recognizing that both ethical values and usability needs must be co-articulated rather than imposed. The user is understood as a co-creator and actively involved in the design process. Both the process and the resulting product are considered equally important, reflecting a commitment to shared responsibility and mutual learning. This aligns with the triadic model and the structured procedure outlined in Chap. 5. It requires the active participation of all relevant stakeholders and experts (Chap. 6). While we recognize that such inclusive processes can be resource intensive, our aim is to briefly outline how they can be designed and integrated into everyday development practices (Chap. 8). By doing so, engineers and managers alike will be better equipped to identify value-relevant questions and decision points without constantly relying on external consultation or time intensive investigations. Ethical deliberation can be—to a certain degree—integrated in development methods. For example, ethical values can be written down in user stories as Halme et al. (2024) suggest before formulating long-term requirements that need to be fulfilled no matter what.

In the case of mountaineering, the concept of the "user" must be understood expansively: it includes not only immediate human users with diverse abilities, backgrounds, and needs but also, in a broader sense, non-human stakeholders such as the environment. Especially in domains like mountain sports and outdoor navigation, the natural world is not just a backdrop but an affected party whose integrity must be factored into design considerations. Ethical design thus entails developing systems that are sensitive not only to human safety and autonomy but also to ecological responsibility and sustainability.

7.4.4 Discursive Approach: Judging Together

When addressing the normative claim that values should be systematically and justly incorporated into technological design processes, the methodology of *Value Sensitive Design* (VSD) offers a valuable starting point. VSD integrates conceptual, empirical, and technical investigations to develop value-oriented technological artifacts. An approach closely aligned with the triadic model of ethical design. Yetim (2011) has proposed enhancing VSD through elements of discourse ethics, particularly Jürgen Habermas's theory of communicative action, with the aim of fostering more democratic, reflective, and just decision-making in the design and evaluation of information systems.

This integration underscores the importance of participatory approaches. Discourse ethics, as developed by Habermas (1993) and Nida-Rümelin (2016), offers practical normative orientation for participatory design by structuring the meta-criteria of dialogue emphasizing truthfulness, reliability, and trust as foundational principles.

The deliberative phase, which forms the normative core of the design process, involves evaluating and prioritizing previously identified values, goal conflicts, and potential courses of action through participatory negotiation. While traditional VSD lacks formal mechanisms for structuring such deliberation, discourse ethics offers a procedural foundation for normative reasoning and conflict resolution. Habermas distinguishes between three types of practical discourse: pragmatic discourse, concerned with means-end reasoning; ethical discourse, focused on what is good for individuals or groups; and moral discourse, which seeks universally justifiable norms. Principles such as the *principle of universalization* and the *appropriateness principle* provide standards for validating outcomes. Here ethical theories become relevant (Chap. 4). Through this process, stakeholders are empowered to critically reflect on their assumptions, values, and interests in relation to others, ultimately working toward a shared will.

These types of discourse and normative principles can be applied concretely in the design of an avalanche safety app. For example, a pragmatic discourse might address which technical solutions (e.g., real-time GPS tracking or automated risk notifications) are most effective for ensuring timely alerts. An ethical discourse would consider the value of *autonomy*, whether it is good for users to retain freedom of movement despite risks or whether more prescriptive safety measures are desirable. A moral discourse would involve a broader negotiation of justice, asking whether it is fair to restrict access to avalanche-prone areas for the sake of public safety and under what conditions such restrictions can be universally justified. The principle of universalization would require that any resulting norm such as

7.4 Deliberative Decision-Making Phase: Navigating Ethical Disagreement

location-based access control could be accepted by all affected parties without coercion, while the appropriateness principle would ensure that this norm is context sensitive, accounting for local practices, risk perceptions, and infrastructural realities. In this way, discourse ethics not only guides the process of deliberation but also shapes the structure of legitimate, value-sensitive technology design.

Participatory processes guided by discourse ethics foster moral legitimacy, context sensitivity, and awareness. They ensure that the values embedded in digital technologies are not simply projected by developers but co-constructed through processes that respect pluralism, vulnerability, and interdependence. Only through such participatory, dialogical, and inclusive practices can technologies like digital avalanche safety management apps truly embody values like truthfulness, responsibility, modesty, care, autonomy, and sustainability, supporting not just individual well-being but the resilience of social and ecological systems alike.

While ethically reflective design processes strive for inclusivity and value sensitivity, it is important to acknowledge a practical critique. Ethical deliberation often leads to greater complexity in products, making them potentially less streamlined, harder to use, or more demanding for users. When multiple, sometimes conflicting values are embedded into design, tensions can arise that complicate user experience rather than simplifying it. Ethical design may also introduce more critical interaction points. Rather than guiding users along a frictionless path, it may ask them to reflect, choose, and bear responsibility, which can be cognitively or emotionally burdensome. Against this background, it is important to recognize that ethical deliberation does not require addressing all possible values or accommodating all user abilities at once. Rather, a responsible approach should clearly articulate which values are prioritized, which user needs are supported, and which perspectives or abilities are consciously and transparently left outside the core design focus. This honesty about scope and limitations does not diminish ethical responsibility; on the contrary, it strengthens it by preventing false inclusivity claims and by making the design choices visible, contestable, and open to future revision. Ethical deliberation, then, should not aim for the impossible ideal of total inclusivity and value coverage but for transparent, justified prioritizations that respect pluralism while maintaining practical usability.

While discourse ethics provides procedural criteria for the justification of norms, such as the principle of universalization and the appropriateness principle, it does not claim to offer ultimate or foundational justifications (*Letztbegründungen*) in the classical metaphysical sense. Ethical and moral reasoning, particularly in complex sociotechnical contexts, is inherently fallible, situated, and open to revision. Rather than seeking fixed truths, discourse ethics emphasizes the procedural legitimacy of norms: what matters is not the absolute truth of a norm but whether it could be justified in an open, inclusive, and rational discourse among all those affected.

This has significant implications for ethical software design: instead of grounding design decisions in fixed moral truths, the emphasis shifts toward fostering *ongoing dialogue, reflexive engagement*, and *revisable consensus*. In the case of the avalanche safety app, for instance, decisions about restricting access or collecting sensitive location data are not resolved through timeless moral principles but through revisable agreements negotiated among stakeholders. These agreements gain provisional legitimacy only insofar as they can be rationally defended in discourse and are open to contestation as values, technologies, and social contexts evolve.

7.4.5 Ethical Dialogue in Teams

In deliberative processes related to discourse ethics, it is essential to include a broad and diverse range of participants to ensure ethically robust and democratically legitimate outcomes. At the core are stakeholders, both direct and indirect. Direct stakeholders are those who interact with the technology directly such as users, planners, or designers, while indirect stakeholders may not use the system themselves but are still affected by its consequences, such as community members or social circles of primary users.

The description of an ethical case is an ongoing process. In Chap. 6, we identified ethically relevant values: a task supported by a diverse group of contributors, each bringing their unique expertise and perspective to the discussion. Company representatives such as compliance officers, CSR managers, and ethics advisors helped align product decisions with internal values, social commitments, and reputational considerations, especially in ethically tense situations like balancing usability and explainability. Legal experts, including data protection officers and legal scholars, ensured that ethical decisions remained within regulatory boundaries and translated abstract principles into legally viable design constraints. Context experts from fields like geology, snow science, and alpine safety grounded the ethical deliberation in the real-world environment of mountain sports, ensuring relevance to actual risks and terrain dynamics. Technology experts, including developers and UX designers, identified technical vulnerabilities and helped design safeguards. End users, particularly skiers, contributed practical insights about everyday use, expectations, and potential misuse. Local communities and environmental experts ensured the technology respected place-based values and promoted sustainability. Ethicists and interdisciplinary moderators played a key role in surfacing blind spots, challenging assumptions, and facilitating inclusive, forward-looking ethical dialogue across all domains involved.

When it comes to making concrete decisions, such as what to prioritize or how to resolve trade-offs, the structure changes. External experts, like those in geology or alpine safety, are typically not involved in final decision-making. Instead, these choices depend on how the company and its development processes are organized internally, often placing decision-making authority in the hands of product teams, managers, or executives.

However, according to the discourse principle, norms are only valid if all affected parties could accept them in a practical discourse. Therefore, the definition of relevance must itself be open to critique. It is important to emphasize that we advocate for a Western understanding of freedom, reason, and responsibility. Approaches that risk undermining individual autonomy or fail to uphold the principles enshrined in the Universal Declaration of Human Rights can automatically be considered incompatible with an open and inclusive dialogue.

The process should empower those affected to determine who may represent their interests. Participants in such discourse are not passive; they actively engage in argumentative exchange, adopt the perspectives of others, and work toward forming a jointly supported judgment. In the face of value conflicts, they reflect on which values matter and explore which design options are acceptable to all involved. The technology experts should open up to include the public, as those who must live with the consequences of design decisions. In this view, users are not merely consulted at the start of a project but are engaged throughout its lifecycle, particularly as new stakeholders and unforeseen value tensions emerge.

Group dynamics also play a role in discourse ethics. Within stakeholder groups, divergent perceptions and interpretations can spark internal discussions and negotiations, enhancing the depth and legitimacy of the discourse. To facilitate such complex, multi-perspective dialogues, moderators or facilitators are crucial. They structure the conversation, synthesize contributions, highlight disagreements, and maintain tools like discourse maps. Importantly, they are themselves participants in the collaborative inquiry process. Finally, practitioners, those driving the design process, are encouraged to critically examine the boundaries they assume in their projects. They can help initiate relevant discourses and support more informed and inclusive decision-making.

However, when decisiveness is understood as a virtue, it is not merely a cognitive process but rather an attitudinal orientation toward the world. As such, it cannot be fully captured through rational deliberation alone but must be cultivated through practice. The development of this kind of decisiveness requires repeated exposure to situations that demand it. Therefore, it is essential to foster decisiveness in specific domains by deliberately placing individuals in environments where such decisions must continually be made. This form of contextual training helps build not only the habit of decision-making but also the underlying disposition to act decisively and responsibly under conditions of uncertainty or conflict.

References

Gibbard, A. (1990). *Wise choices, apt feelings: A theory of normative judgment.* Harvard University Press.
Gogoll, J., Zuber, N., Kacianka, S., Greger, T., Pretschner, A., & Nida-Rümelin, J. (2021). Ethics in the software development process: From codes of conduct to ethical deliberation. *Philosophy & Technology, 34*(4), 1085–1108.
Habermas, J. (1993). *Die Einbeziehung des Anderen: Studien zur politischen Theorie.* Suhrkamp Taschenbuch Wissenschaft.

Halme, E., Jantunen, M., Vakkuri, V., Kemell, K. K., & Abrahamsson, P. (2024). Making ethics practical: User stories as a way of implementing ethical consideration in Software Engineering. *Information and Software Technology, 167*, Article 107379. https://doi.org/10.1016/j.infsof.2023.107379

Jonsen, A. R., Toulmin, S., & Toulmin, S. E. (1988). *The abuse of casuistry: A history of moral reasoning.* University of California Press.

Jonas, H. (1979). *Das Prinzip Verantwortung: Versuch einer Ethik für die technologische Zivilisation.* Suhrkamp Verlag.

Leopold, A. (1970). *A sand county Almanac.* Ballantine. (Original work published 1949).

Nagel, T. (1979). *Mortal questions.* Cambridge University Press.

Nida-Rümelin, J. (2016). *Humanistische Reflexionen.* Suhrkamp Verlag.

Nida-Rümelin, J. (2023). *A theory of practical reason.* Palgrave Macmillan.

O'Neill, O. (2003). Autonomy: The emperor's new clothes. *Aristotelian Society Supplementary, 77*(1), 1–21.

Rawls, J. (1971). *A theory of justice: Original edition.* Harvard University Press. https://doi.org/10.2307/j.ctvjf9z6v

Yetim, F. (2008). Critical examination of information: A discursive approach and its implementations. *Informing Science, 11*, 125–146.

Yetim, F. (2011). Bringing discourse ethics to value sensitive design: Pathways toward a deliberative future. *AIS Transactions on Human-Computer Interaction, 3*(2), 133–155.

Zuber, N., Gogoll, J., Kacianka, S., Pretschner, A., & Nida-Rümelin, J. (2022). Empowered and embedded: Ethics and agile processes. *Humanities and Social Sciences Communications, 9*(1), 1–13.

Open Access   This chapter is licensed under the terms of the Creative Commons Attribution 4.0 International License (http://creativecommons.org/licenses/by/4.0/), which permits use, sharing, adaptation, distribution and reproduction in any medium or format, as long as you give appropriate credit to the original author(s) and the source, provide a link to the Creative Commons license and indicate if changes were made.

The images or other third party material in this chapter are included in the chapter's Creative Commons license, unless indicated otherwise in a credit line to the material. If material is not included in the chapter's Creative Commons license and your intended use is not permitted by statutory regulation or exceeds the permitted use, you will need to obtain permission directly from the copyright holder.

Chapter 8
Organization, People and Processes

> "We may as well assert, that a man, by remaining in a vessel, freely consents to the dominion of the master; though he was carried on board while asleep, and must leap into the ocean, and perish, the moment he leaves her"
>
> (Hume, 1770)

Abstract This chapter highlights the crucial role organizational structures play in enabling ethical deliberation within software development. It emphasizes that ethical software engineering depends not only on deliberating about what is right but also on creating an organizational structure that actively supports ethical reflection and decision-making. Ethical deliberation cannot properly flourish in environments constrained by tight deadlines, inadequate resources, or conflicting incentives; therefore, organizations must intentionally cultivate both formal and informal structures that promote ethical awareness and deliberation. Furthermore, this chapter argues that agile methodologies offer a particularly conducive environment for ethical deliberation through their iterative processes, team autonomy, and low hierarchies. Specifically, Sprint 0 and the role of the Product Owner are identified as a key point and role for integrating ethics early and continuously into the development process. Ultimately, the chapter calls for institutionalizing ethical practices within software-producing organizations, acknowledging the uniqueness of each organizational context, and underscoring the necessity of adapting these guidelines pragmatically to achieve sustainable ethical software development.

While David Hume (1994/1770) originally penned these words about political authority, the insight is just as relevant in the corridors of modern organizations. Authority takes many forms, and in the realm of software development, the "master" may often be the organizational structure itself. Having read this book up to this point will hopefully provide the interested developer or manager with some tools to spot and address ethical issues and deliberate about them, but without the resources, time, and incentives to support such deliberations, that capability may be as illusory (or at least prohibitively expensive) as the sailor's supposed choice to jump into the ocean. It is not enough to give developers the skills they need to do the right thing while binding them with tight deadlines, inadequate resources, or incentives that may push them into the other direction. To truly enable ethical software development, organizations need to provide an environment where deliberation is not only possible but encouraged—because no one should have to metaphorically *leap into the ocean* to be able to address ethical issues in software development. After all, the goal is to create *good* software.

A fundamental truth about ethical deliberation within an organizational context is: no matter how comprehensive or well-intentioned the ethical guidelines, codes of conduct, or best practices might be, they will struggle to take root in an organization that lacks the right culture and structure—in short, will—to support them. Ethical software engineering is not just about defining what is right or wrong (and what this book has talked about thus far); it's also about building an environment where ethical reasoning becomes a natural part of everyday decision-making. In this sense, it mirrors a form of virtue ethics, as discussed in Chap. 4, but applied to organizations. Organizations should be designed as spaces where *doing the right thing* is encouraged—a culture that supports ethical reflection, with internal incentives that enable and foster ethical discussions and actions or at least not be an impediment to them.

Of course, this is not to suggest a naïve stance in which ethics should always take precedence over all other reasons. Particularly in commercial settings, software development is shaped by systemic constraints: time to market, competitive pressure, and the imperative to meet user or client demand. These are legitimate reasons and drivers of organizational behavior and part of their raison d'être. However, they are not sufficient in themselves to justify every decision, nor do the means always justify the ends.

In our view, ethical deliberation must be integrated in a way that is both principled and pragmatic. It would be unreasonable to expect that organizations regularly sacrifice economic sustainability in order to satisfy the mirage of a perfect ethical decision. At the same time, treating ethics as entirely subordinate to profit motives undermines the long-term trust, credibility, and legitimacy that organizations rely on. Just as ethical software design requires phronesis—practical wisdom—(Chap. 7) in balancing competing values, so too does the organization need phronesis in deciding how much time, energy, and resources to invest in ethical reflection and safeguards. It is not about perfect solutions but about making responsible, context-sensitive judgments.

Take the case of Amazon's AI-based recruitment tool, which was discovered to exhibit bias against female candidates due to the fact that the historic data on which it was trained happened to have overwhelmingly males in leadership roles. Despite its technical sophistication, the lack of a proper structure to address ethical concerns during development led the tool to perpetuate gender biases—a flaw that came to light only after the project was almost completed, with significant resources already invested and—thus—wasted. Similarly, in the Facebook-Cambridge Analytica scandal, Facebook's prioritization of growth and engagement over privacy concerns resulted in the misuse of user data on a massive scale. In both cases, the lack of an organizational environment that supported ethical deliberation led to outcomes that violated ethical values, underscoring the importance of proper structures for ethical software development.

In this chapter, we explore the often-overlooked but crucial role of organizational structure in enabling ethical deliberation within software development. While much of the existing literature tends to focus on the *what* of ethical engineering—articulating values, norms, and principles and applying them to software artifacts—the *how* of implementing these values within an organization is frequently neglected. This structural aspect, as Blackman (2022) aptly describes as "content" versus "structure," plays a pivotal role in ensuring that ethical considerations are not just theoretical ideals but are actively integrated into the software development process.

By examining the human and organizational factors that shape ethical software development, we delve into how teams, departments, and entire organizations can foster an environment conducive to ethical decision-making. In short, this chapter explores both formal and informal mechanisms that foster and cultivate ethical behavior within organizations. These levers help guide the promotion and development of moral conduct across different organizational levels. Without this foundation, even the most well-defined ethical principles risk becoming mere aspirations, unable to guide the design and implementation of normatively well-designed software. What we need and thus should aim for is an *institutionalization* of ethics and, to make it happen, an *organizational Buy-In*. Of course, people may leverage "narratives of regulatory response and ethics as product quality assurance" (Ahlawat et al., 2024) to get ethical issues taken seriously by using instrumental arguments. Ideally, however, individuals with decision-making authority should emphasize that voicing ethical concerns is as essential to the development process as identifying technical impediments.

8.1 The Essential Role of (Organizational) Structure

Ethics in software engineering entails a dual focus: First, the ethical reasoning surrounding the product and its application (this book so far) in the form of ethical deliberations and decisions, codes of conduct, checklists, or best practices and, second, the organizational structure that enables and fosters this ethical reasoning. While the former concerns the ethical features of the product itself, the latter addresses the mechanisms within the organization that facilitate the necessary ethical discourse and enable designers, engineers, and management to spot, deliberate on, decide, and ultimately implement ethical choices into good software.

This distinction has largely taken a backseat in the literature, which often emphasizes value statements and their implementation or outsources ethical concerns to committees like ethics boards. The human factor that needs to be empowered and enabled in order to implement and conduct ethical deliberation within the software development process tends to receive, with a few exceptions notwithstanding, implicit recognition at best. In other words, it focuses on *what* to do and neglects, in large parts, *how* to do it or, in other words, the role of context in which software development happens. Of course, this distinction is not new and well-known in management and organizational studies.

The *content* side of ethical deliberation in software engineering involves an examination of a product's specific attributes, their associated ethical values, and potential benefits. It answers the fundamental normative question of how the product ought to be designed and implemented (see Chaps. 6 and 7). Therefore, this dimension should involve an active deliberation process aimed at shaping the product's design in ways that enhance its moral value or prevent the deterioration of its normative or functional worth. This practical reasoning deals with identifying relevant normative issues as well as balancing potential trade-offs between two or more competing ethical values. This endeavor is normative in nature since its results provide guidance, yet "it would be odd that crucial empirical findings about human motivation, organizational behavior, norm-induced attitudes, etc., should have no normative implications" (Francés-Gómez et al., 2015). Thus, the *structure* side of ethical software development needs to be taken into consideration. The task of ethical deliberation in organization builds on human action, including the participation of a diverse group of individuals, such as software developers, designers, managerial staff, and various stakeholders. The success of such an endeavor is contingent upon a multitude of factors, which can be conceptualized as necessary conditions that facilitate the initial commencement of ethical deliberations. To really appreciate the *structure* side of ethical software development, we must put an emphasis on the human factor perspective: software development is usually a social activity—performed in teams with members of various expertise, within departments and, finally, within organizations (Chaps. 6 and 7). To ensure that an ethical deliberation and decisions on concrete design and its implementation (the content) actually take place with the appropriate effort and resources, we need to address the environment that the developers and designers find themselves in—including the factors of an informal kind, e.g., organizational (ethical) climate as well as formal factors, which, for instance, include incentives and time and resource constraints regarding deliberation and implementation efforts. Some have made the distinction between individual factors (e.g., moral awareness, [personal] moral development, etc.) and situational factors, which are defined as "forces [that] represent the situational pressures which come to bear on the individual to encourage or discourage ethical decision making" (Ford & Richardson, 1994). The *structure* side of ethical software development could be, in simple terms, described as getting the right people in an ethics supportive environment. Thus we have two factors on the structural side that may help or hinder ethical awareness and deliberation: The individuals who work at creating software products and the organizations resp. the structure of these organizations in which they do so.

Similar to Kant's *ought-implies-can* principle, which holds that moral obligations are only meaningful if a person has the capacity and ability to fulfill them, the governance of an organization must allow and support ethical deliberation for it to be effective. While this is a less strict interpretation of the principle—since it's not entirely impossible for developers to engage in ethical deliberation even if the organization provides no resources or actively discourages it—it highlights that without support, opportunities, or sufficient time to address ethical concerns, successful implementation becomes reliant on extraordinary individual efforts or sheer luck, something that would rely on what ethicists call a *supererogatory* act or *moral heroism*. In such environments, ethical deliberation may occur only through the exceptional actions of certain engineers, but this places an undue burden on them and therefore does not present itself as a sensible strategy. A weaker interpretation of "ability" suggests that any ethical demands on an employee must be similarly weaker, as the costs of engaging in ethical deliberation—such as the risk of losing one's job or forgoing a promotion—can be prohibitively high. Behavioral and organizational science has produced a vast amount of research that identifies features of organizations and the individuals working within an organizational framework that foster relevant features like autonomous thinking, (moral) motivation, and opportunity by providing proper incentives and resources. The interplay of these conditions significantly influences the feasibility and effectiveness of conducting proper ethical considerations.

8.1.1 Ethical Software Development as an Organizational Endeavor

Software development is commonly executed within organizations. Studying the implementation of ethical deliberation within organizations thus holds significant importance as it encompasses a distinct set of dynamics. Organizations are hierarchical by definition as they provide decision rights to some members but not others in order to facilitate collective decision-making (Athey & Roberts, 2001). These decision rights are usually at the top level of an organization but may be temporarily delegated to lower levels—creating downstream leaders and followers. They include the rights to hire, fire, pricing, advertising, and—most importantly for our purposes—determining operating procedures such as processes and product design (Brief & Smith-Crowe, 2016).

Individuals operating in organizational contexts must therefore navigate power structures, authority hierarchies, and peer influences—all of which may vary between organizations and times but shape the individual's actions and have an impact on their decision-making processes. Treviño et al. (2014) highlight the "powerful influence of peers, leaders, significant others, rules, laws, and codes," which can all "guide employees' ethical decision making and behavior" (ibid.). By examining this context, we realize how these organizational factors impact behavior and moral deliberation. Understanding the interplay between individuals and their organizational environment can help provide a comprehensive understanding of how one can foster ethical product development within organizations. This can mean two things: the avoidance of unwanted normative outcomes and the furthering of normatively better products.

Highlighting the difference between the ethical behaviors of individuals and those of organizations is essential in understanding the complexities of ethical decision-making. Placing exclusive emphasis on individual actions might lead to what is known as the *atomistic fallacy* (Alker Jr, 1969). This fallacy assumes that ethical conduct at the individual level will inevitably translate into an ethical organizational culture. However, an organization is more than the sum of its parts; it comprises intricate systems, hierarchies, groups, and structures that can either enable or constrain ethical behavior. To solely concentrate on individual behavior while neglecting the broader organizational context overlooks the intricate interplay between formal structures, leadership dynamics, and the collective ethical climate of an organization. It is by recognizing and addressing these systemic elements that an organization can authentically foster ethical values and practices from the ground up. This means that understanding the intricate ethical dynamics within organizations requires a nuanced perspective that acknowledges both the individual and collective dimensions (Ford & Richardson, 1994).

This also means that if one is serious about a consistent and fruitful implementation of ethical deliberation within software development, an organizational commitment is necessary.

This subsection thus delves briefly into the behavioral findings regarding ethical behavior within organizations, highlighting the formal and informal elements that constitute the foundation for effective ethical software development. Drawing from established research in behavioral ethics, this section lists the multifaceted impact of organizational contexts on individuals' ethical behavior, emphasizing the significance of ethical climate and ethical culture as influential factors. These often manifest themselves in the form of work processes, which will be discussed in the main part of this article. Some have also used the term "ethical infrastructures" to refer to the structural features of an organization that fosters or hinders ethical deliberation and action (Tenbrunsel et al., 2003).

Treviño et al. (2006) state that it is clear "that the task of designing organizations to foster ethical behavior is not always a straightforward and simple one," yet the behavioral and organizational ethics literature has identified some patterns of structure that seem to be connected to an increase in ethical awareness, decision-making, and behavior. Regarding the ethical deliberation and its requirements, it seems that "providing the structures that facilitate such deliberation: physical space; time for introspection and reflection; organization of meetings dedicated to organizational objectives and workplace practices; identification of issues on which decisions need to be made; and attention devoted to the different ways of doing good should be initialized in order for it to be successful" (Frémeaux & Voegtlin, 2023). The development process thus seems to be a good place to incorporate ethical deliberation as it is here where requirements are determined and trade-offs chosen.

8.1.2 Intra-, Inter-, and Organizational Level

Ethical behavior within organizations is a complex and multifaceted concept that encompasses not only individual choices and actions but also the broader organizational context in which these behaviors occur. Scholars and researchers in the field of organizational ethics have consistently emphasized the significance of organizational structure as a determinant of ethical conduct (e.g., Treviño et al., 2014; De Cremer & Moore, 2020). Here we will explore the distinctions commonly made in

8.1 The Essential Role of (Organizational) Structure

the literature between intrapersonal, interpersonal (sometimes called contextual (Jackson et al., 2013)), and organizational levels of analysis. Each of these three levels of analysis contains elements that collectively influence the way ethical issues are tackled within a corporation. These factors should be seen as a convergence that exerts an influence on individuals or groups when they are making ethical choices or a sequence of ethical choices and whether these choices are understood to have ethical relevance in the first place (Table 8.1).

Table 8.1 Ethical software development at the intra-, inter-, and organizational levels

Level	Description	Key elements	Example
Intrapersonal level	Focuses on individual cognition, affective processes, and personal differences that shape ethical behavior	• Cognitive processes (moral perception and judgment) • Affective processes (emotional responses) • Personality traits • Personal values • Education	A developer has a personal dedication to privacy and actively tries to increase that value by choosing a fitting implementation
Interpersonal level	Concerns the influence of leadership, power dynamics, and peer interaction on ethical decision-making within groups and teams	• Ethical leadership • Power dynamics and decision rights • Agency of low-power holders • Peer influence and social proximity • Group discussion	A junior developer, initially reluctant to raise concerns about privacy concerns regarding an algorithm, speaks up after a team leader encourages open discussion of ethical issues
Organizational level	Encompasses the structural and cultural factors within an organization that collectively shape the ethical climate and influence behavior	• Ethical climate (shared norms and perceptions) • Ethical culture (formal/informal elements) • Top management (tone setting) • Ethical codes and resources	A tech company introduces a mandatory pre-sprint workshop in which stakeholders and team members identify potential ethical concerns, moderated by an ethics expert to ensure structured reflection and shared accountability before development begins

While individual cognition and moral development differences between individuals may not fall squarely within the organizational realm, it is imperative to acknowledge the significance of these variables as drivers of ethical deliberation and decision-making within organizations.

At the *intrapersonal* level, ethical behavior is shaped by a range of cognitive and affective processes as well as individual differences among employees. Cognitive processes involve the way individuals perceive ethical issues, process information, and make moral judgments. In Chap. 6, we discussed how to identify ethical issues; however, even with an objective methodological approach, individual perspectives and differences still play a significant role. Affective processes, on the other hand, encompass emotional responses to ethical situations, which can influence an individual's ethical decision-making. Moreover, individual differences, including personality traits, personal values, and moral development, play a significant role in determining how employees approach and navigate ethical challenges. Additionally, education plays a role regarding ethical competence as does exposure to deliberate ethical decisions during employment (Smith and Kouchaki (2021). These intrapersonal factors interact with the organizational structure to either reinforce or challenge an individual's commitment to ethical behavior. Motivation constitutes a central factor in ethical behavior, as it determines whether moral insight translates into action. While cognitive and affective processes shape how individuals recognize and evaluate ethical issues, motivation sustains the intention to act in accordance with one's judgment. It thereby addresses the classical problem of *akrasia*—the weakness of will—where individuals fail to do what they know to be right. Ethical motivation is, however, not a given; it requires the continuous integration of moral conviction, emotional engagement, and self-regulatory capacity. Cultivating and maintaining such motivation is a complex psychological achievement that depends on the interplay between moral reasoning, affective resonance, and the individual's sense of responsibility and integrity (see De Cremer & Moore 2020).

Beyond individual traits, ethical behavior is also deeply shaped by the teams and leaders surrounding a developer—this is the *interpersonal* level. It seems prima facie clear that ethical decision-making is influenced by several critical factors, including—but not limited to—ethical leadership, power resp. decision rights, and the agency of low-power holders or followers to speak up. Ethical leadership, exemplified by managers and supervisors, sets the tone for ethical conduct within an organization. Leaders who model ethical behavior and communicate clear ethical expectations can positively influence the ethical behavior and motivation of their subordinates. Power dynamics within an organization also play a crucial role in interpersonal ethics. The distribution of power and decision rights affects how individuals interact with one another, and those in positions of power can significantly impact the ethical climate. Furthermore, recognizing the agency of low-power holders is essential. Empowering employees with limited authority to voice their ethical concerns and contribute to decision-making processes can enhance overall interpersonal ethical behavior. Software development is often conducted in small groups, e.g., in agile processes consisting of a development team, a scrum master, and a product owner (PO). Therefore, decisions within this greater team are subjected to peer influences. The effect of peer influence on moral decision-making is well established in the literature (Yu et al., 2021). Dimant (2019) speaks of the "contagion of pro-and anti-social behavior" given social proximity among peers. A single member of the group may significantly influence the choices and preferences of other members (Dijksterhuis & Aarts, 2010), and the goal-oriented desires of others cause those objectives to become more prominent for oneself, which may amplify the significance of attributes aligned with those goals in decision-making, including ethical decisions via goals that are ethics oriented (Yu et al., 2021). People observe others' behavior and orient themselves due to in-group dynamics. In fact, experimental evidence suggests that active conversation and contemplation about ethical issues within groups have a significant effect on ethical behavior as compared to immediate choice (Gunia et al., 2012). Procedural steps that might be implemented into organizational decision-making thus offer a promising option in order to increase ethical salience of software design. One important aspect is leadership and what can be called "tone from the top." When strategies are selected and actions are taken by an organization, these strategies and actions are, of course, made by individuals within the organization. The individuals most influential in determining these actions are the organization's top managers. These individuals have the requisite power and resources along with the responsibility to develop and implement organizational processes through which their expectations can be carried out. Top management in its normative selections and normative commitments (Mitnick, 1995) sets the moral tone for the organization and is primarily responsible for establishing and maintaining the moral climate of the organization. (See Cohen (1995) for a review of this literature.)

At the ***organizational*** **level**, ethical behavior pertains to the collective actions and decisions of the organization as a whole and how these affect the individuals and groups who work within it. This includes the development and enforcement of ethical policies and practices. To make this more understandable, it can be useful to distinguish between *formal* and *informal* factors. While this distinction is not always perfectly clear-cut—there are often gray areas—it serves to highlight the difference between what can be more directly influenced (such as policies or procedures) and what needs to evolve naturally through informal cultural elements within the organization (ethical climate, the "*way* we do things here"). Formal systems within an organization refer to clearly defined, documented actions and procedures within an organization that are specifically designed to promote ethical behavior. These visible mechanisms serve as the structural backbone to enable ethical deliberations to take place. Yet many forms of formal organizational control systems (a classic management approach) focus on defined objectives, monitoring, and sanctions. Although they can help deter immoral behavior, they do not necessarily encourage moral behavior, as their focus lies in discouraging actions already recognized as unethical. Control systems thus are of little use when it comes to encouraging ethical deliberation.

In contrast to formal systems, informal systems in an organization encompass all the uncodified and less visible elements that influence behavior. These are not predetermined or explicitly documented policies or practices. Rather, they include unwritten norms, shared organizational patterns, and the influence of role models within the company. Additionally, informal systems involve rituals, stories, and even specific language or jargon that employees use, which collectively shape the ethical atmosphere of the organization. These elements grow organically over time, creating an environment where ethics is practiced not just through rules but through the lived experiences and day-to-day interactions of the organization's members. Such informal dynamics play a crucial role in fostering a sustainable ethical culture, as they influence behavior in subtler yet powerful ways. They manifest through everyday interactions, for instance, how openly team members voice concerns, the unwritten norms regarding acceptable trade-offs, or whether raising ethical issues is met with encouragement or resistance. To be more concrete, imagine a development team that habitually discusses ethical considerations during their coffee breaks: this informal practice significantly reinforces ethical deliberation more authentically than mandated procedures alone.

Codes of ethics are often used to this end, although they might be only useful if combined with a proper ethical deliberation about product features (Gogoll et al., 2021). The organizational structure significantly impacts the establishment and implementation of ethical deliberation. For instance, the allocation of resources for ethical deliberation and the inclusion of ethical considerations in strategic planning are all structural elements that can promote ethical behavior at the organizational level. The literature speaks of ethical climate and culture (Treviño et al., 2014). Moreover, the degree of decentralization and the distribution of decision-making authority within an organization can affect its ethical stance. An organization with a decentralized structure may empower individual units to make ethical decisions independently, potentially resulting in variations in ethical behavior across different departments. To counter these variations, a process-focused approach seems sensible.

Ethical software development cannot rely solely on the moral strength of individuals. Without the right structures—processes that integrate ethical reflection into decision-making, leadership that sets the tone from the top, and a culture that values open dialogue about ethical concerns—even the best ethical intentions risk withering under everyday pressures. Organizations must treat ethics not as an optional add-on but as an integral part of how they operate. This means deliberately creating environments where ethical concerns can be voiced early, heard seriously, and acted upon pragmatically. It requires both formal systems (e.g., codes of ethics, resources, and ethical deliberation spaces) and informal aspects (e.g., team norms and leadership behaviors that foster an ethical culture). Yet this is neither a simple nor overnight endeavor. Building structures that genuinely support ethical deliberation demands effort, perseverance, and a willingness to confront organizational inertia. It is a tough demand, one that requires continuous commitment rather than one-time initiatives. Nevertheless, the stakes are too high to ignore. Fostering ethical deliberation is not just about preventing harm or avoiding scandals. It is about ensuring that the technologies we build strengthen, rather than undermine, the trust on which all social life depends.

If we aim to build software that is good, then organizations must recognize ethical reflection as a strength, not a liability. By institutionalizing ethical practices, we transform the burden of individual heroism into a shared organizational commitment—one that is more sustainable and more likely to succeed.

8.2 Leveraging Agile Frameworks for Ethical Deliberation

Software products, like the organizations that create them, are naturally idiosyncratic—each domain, team composition, or technical goal presents unique challenges that resist a single universal formula. Consequently, this book does not attempt to prescribe a one-size-fits-all model of organizational design; rather, it highlights how deliberate structures and cultures are crucial in fostering ethical awareness and action. We maintain that empowering individuals—giving them real decision rights and resources—represents one of the most effective ways to support robust ethical deliberation. Within this context, agile processes often prove especially well suited, as their emphasis on iterative work, team autonomy, and frequent reflection provides fertile ground for ongoing moral consideration.

Agile software development methods provide a promising structural basis to embed ethical reflection and reasoning into day-to-day software development processes. As we have argued above, ethical software development is not only a matter of what to deliberate about (the content side) but also how and where this deliberation happens (the structure side). Agile processes—because of their procedural flexibility, strong emphasis on team participation, and iterative nature—can be seen as a fitting organizational framework to support the structural side of ethics in practice. Rather than viewing ethical deliberation as an additional burden, agile processes offer built-in affordances that can be mobilized to empower normative reflection within everyday development cycles.

But the effectiveness of this development process, and ethical deliberation more broadly, depends on more than just goodwill or individual sensitivity. Ethical deliberation—like any other activity in an organizational setting—requires structural support. As noted in the previous section, ethical obligations that cannot realistically be fulfilled by practitioners due to lack of time, incentive, or authority risk becoming ineffective. Agile structures help mitigate this by providing the necessary organizational affordances for ethics to take root (Zuber et al., 2022).

First, agile is already widely adopted in the software industry. Introducing ethics into an existing, well-understood framework minimizes disruption and increases the chance of adoption. Ethics need not be bolted onto the process; it can be woven into established rituals like sprint planning, retrospectives, refinement meetings, or backlog creation. Because these meetings are already designed to facilitate reflection and course correction, they serve as natural insertion points for value-sensitive deliberation. This also reduces the cost of implementation, as no new meetings or roles are needed—only a reinterpretation of existing ones.

Second, agile promotes flat hierarchies and team autonomy. This structural feature is critical for fostering moral agency among developers. When individuals feel empowered to speak up, question assumptions, and take responsibility for their choices, ethical deliberation becomes possible. Conversely, in rigidly hierarchical organizations where developers are merely executing pre-determined instructions, the opportunity to identify or raise ethical concerns is diminished. Autonomy and responsibility are mutually reinforcing: developers who feel responsible are more likely to think ethically, and those who are structurally empowered are more likely to assume responsibility. Agile's focus on empowerment, peer-to-peer collaboration, and distributed authority directly supports this dynamic.

Third, agile methodologies emphasize the importance of functioning, self-organized teams. Ethical deliberation thrives not in isolation but in dialogue. It requires the confrontation of perspectives, the exchange of reasons, and the negotiation of value conflicts. Agile teams, through their collaborative practices, daily stand-ups, and shared ownership of outcomes, provide the discursive setting in which this can happen. Instead of outsourcing ethics to detached committees or documents, the agile team itself becomes the place where values are recognized, debated, and transformed into product features. This embeddedness helps normalize ethical deliberation as part of the craft, not as an external obligation.

Fourth, the iterative, incremental nature of agile supports what we might call techno-ethical realism. Ethical reasoning becomes anchored in real artifacts, not abstract speculation. Each sprint produces a working increment, which allows ethical concerns to be evaluated in context. This short feedback loop enables ethical hypotheses to be tested, revised, and re-integrated. For example, if a privacy-preserving feature proves too confusing to users, the team can explore more intelligible alternatives in the next iteration. Agile's responsiveness allows normative principles to be stress-tested in practice, helping developers navigate the tension between ideal ethical standards and real-world constraints.

Finally, agile time-boxing offers a psychological and procedural endpoint to ethical deliberation. One of the risks in ethical design is inertia due to excessive deliberation or never-ending debates that delay release. Agile's fixed-length sprints and clearly defined deliverables enforce a stopping rule: within this timeframe, we consider what can be ethically improved, make our best judgment, and move on. This structure encourages satisficing—choosing an option that meets a sufficient level of ethical adequacy rather than chasing perfection. Moreover, it enables continuity: if an ethical concern cannot be fully resolved in one sprint, it can be scheduled for future iterations, ensuring deliberation remains actionable and integrated within the project timeline.

Taken together, these features show that agile is not merely compatible with ethical deliberation—it is, in many respects, conducive to it. Its widespread adoption lowers the entry threshold; its flat hierarchies empower moral agency; its collaborative structures support ethical dialogue; its iteration enables practical realism; and its time-boxing mechanisms provide closure. When these features are taken seriously and supplemented with explicit ethical guidance (e.g., checklists, value canvases, or training), agile can become not just a method for rapid development but a platform for cultivating reflective, responsible, and ethically grounded software practices.

The structural side of ethics—often neglected in the literature on software ethics—finds a promising ally in agile methods. By providing the organizational preconditions under which ethical awareness and deliberation can flourish, agile has the ability to foster the "ought implies can" environment that ethical software development requires. The Product Owner, as a central orchestrator of priorities and stakeholder values, becomes a key actor in this system—facilitating not only functional progress but also the integration of normative insight into the software development lifecycle.

8.2.1 Mapping Agile to Ethical Deliberation

Integrating ethics into agile is about building on existing ceremonies and artifacts, rather than adding heavy new processes—this is the reason why we mention the agile method at this point. Of course agile methods are not a necessary condition to implement ethical deliberation into software development—many other frameworks can lead to meaningful outcomes. However, as mentioned above, we believe agile aligns particularly well with this goal and has the added advantage of already being widely adopted in practice (Zuber et al., 2024). A key strategy is to embed ethical checkpoints into the regular agile cadence—infusing ethical deliberation into backlog grooming, sprint planning, reviews, and retrospectives. This approach lowers the implementation costs and reduces the entry barriers to ethical practice, making it more feasible and less disruptive than introducing entirely new processes. The following section offers a brief overview of how the agile framework can be leveraged to support ethically informed software development. We will examine the key ceremonies and roles within the agile framework and outline how each can contribute to ethical deliberation.

Figure 8.1 illustrates this flow, showing where ethical *identification*, *deliberation*, and *evaluation* activities may be implemented into the Scrum workflow without fundamentally altering its structure. Our brief discussion, however, will concentrate primarily on Sprint 0 as the central ceremony and on the Product Owner as the pivotal role.

8.2.2 Sprint 0: Unofficial but Essential for Ethical Deliberation

Agile methodologies define distinct roles and ceremonies, each of which can contribute meaningfully to ethical system development. Interestingly and somewhat ironically, we believe that much of the crucial work involved in *spotting the right*

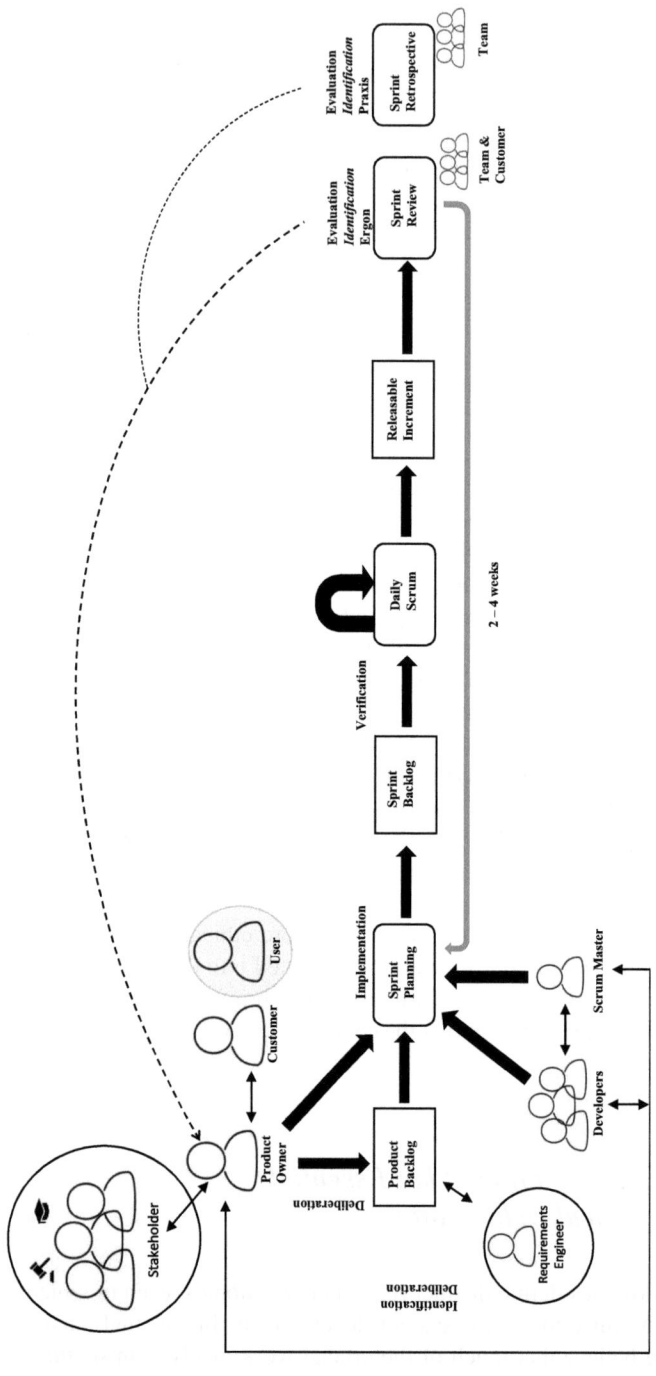

Fig. 8.1 The SCRUM process with added elements for ethical deliberation

(Chap. 6) and aspects of *deciding for the good* (Chap. 7) often occurs during what is commonly referred to as Sprint 0 (sometimes also called the inception sprint or kickoff sprint), which is not an official part of the SCRUM framework. Yet Sprint 0 is widely practiced and plays a foundational role in setting the stage for development (Branco, 2024). It is commonly adopted as a preliminary phase dedicated to planning, alignment, and foundational decision-making before formal development cycles begin. Its typical objectives include assembling or aligning the team, establishing the development environment, articulating the project vision and initial requirements, and creating a preliminary product backlog. We believe it is essential to lay the foundation for ethical development during the initial planning in Sprint 0 and to use the recurring sprints and product increments as opportunities to assess whether we are still on the right track—or whether something previously overlooked has come to light during development. That said, the initial deliberation about which values to prioritize is a foundational aspect of ethical software design and, ideally, should remain mostly stable throughout the sprint cycles. It seems only natural to place ethical analysis at the very beginning of the development process, as questions of value and ethics are typically fundamental and shape the entire vision of what is to be built. Moreover, as discussed in Chap. 6, the epistemic phase or *spotting the right* requires a thorough investigation of the domain for which the artifact is being developed. This step is essential regardless of whether ethical values are explicitly considered, since even from a purely instrumental perspective, it is crucial to understand what is being built, for whom, and how it is intended to function. Acquiring domain knowledge—whether through independent research, consultation with experts, understanding legal frameworks, or involving stakeholders—seems a necessary part of any development process. Integrating questions of domain-specific ethics into this process is therefore a prudent and effective step toward ethically aligned software development. Addressing ethical issues at this point seems only logical, and when done well, Sprint 0 sets up structures that ensure ethics are continually considered in the following development process. This would also alleviate the additional structural challenge for ethical deliberation in digital technology development, as highlighted by scholars such as Olsson and Väänänen (2021), who critique the prevailing reliance on agile development methods and other incremental, iterative processes. In agile development, the focus tends to be on delivering small, continuous improvements through short cycles of prototyping, testing, and refinement. While this methodology enhances responsiveness and adaptability, it often neglects deeper ethical reflection, precisely because it discourages stepping back to critically assess the fundamental assumptions, values, and societal impacts of the system being built. Väänänen argues that, particularly in the age of artificial intelligence, this tendency becomes ethically hazardous because development is structured only around localized optimizations. Hence, there is little space to ask foundational questions about the technology's goals, value commitments, and broader societal consequences. Instead, ethical concerns risk being fragmented into minor usability tweaks or surface-level compliance measures, without addressing the underlying architectures of power and responsibility. Thus, she calls for dedicated methodologies for foundational ethical deliberation processes that periodically disrupt the momentum of incrementalism to re-examine core design choices in light of evolving social, ecological, and normative contexts. Without such structural interventions, even participatory and value-sensitive intentions may fail to penetrate the deeper layers of system design where long-term ethical consequences are shaped. However, taking Sprint 0 into account makes long-term consideration possible.

It is especially important to note that the Product Owner, domain experts, the client, users, and other stakeholders collaboratively bring together all necessary information through discursive processes, enabling informed ethical judgment (Chap. 6). The decision is then typically made based on this discussion, most often by the client and the Product Owner (Chap. 8). However, this does not mean that software engineers are exempt from ethical responsibility during development: they may need to evaluate increments against these requirements or raise awareness if they encounter ethically relevant aspects or alternative solutions.

8.2.3 Product Owner: Orchestrating Ethical Deliberation

While Sprint 0 offers an ideal opportunity to anchor ethical considerations, we see the Product Owner as the role best positioned to integrate ethical deliberation into the agile workflow. Within contemporary agile practice, the Product Owner (PO) occupies the central position at which organizational purpose, stakeholder expectation, and technical execution converge. Scrum literature sometimes labels the role as "Mini-CEO," (Partogi, 2015) and the metaphor is apt: The "Product Owner is empowered to do the right thing by the higher-level management" (scrum.org, 2025) and thus has the necessary decision rights that are paramount in any organization as we discussed above. Within the Scrum framework, the Product Owner is conceived as the single locus of accountability for the value that a team delivers: every feature that enters the Product Backlog, every priority ordering, and every decision to release ultimately flow through this role. The Product Owner plays a pivotal role in articulating the underlying rationale for each user story or planned feature, trying to consolidate disparate stakeholder requests into a coherent and prioritized backlog. The role is thus serving as the critical intermediary between customer needs and the engineers' technical acceptance criteria. As shown in the illustration above, the Product Owner occupies a central position in the communication and coordination flow between stakeholders, customers, users, and the development team. As the one responsible for translating external expectations and stakeholder demands into the product backlog, the Product Owner becomes the linchpin for identifying and prioritizing ethically relevant requirements. Ethical issues do not arise in a vacuum—they emerge from particular contexts, stakeholder needs, and potential tensions between values. It is through the Product Owner that many of these concerns can be initially spotted, articulated, and included in the backlog as items for deliberation. In this way, the Product Owner serves as an

8.2 Leveraging Agile Frameworks for Ethical Deliberation

interface between external moral expectations and internal design decisions, shaping how values get negotiated, prioritized, and operationalized.

In Sprint 0 of an avalanche safety app, the product owner, stakeholders, and domain experts collaboratively engage in structured ethical deliberation before development begins. This process includes identifying critical functionalities such as real-time hazard alerts, route recommendations, and data-sharing mechanisms and examining the associated ethical concerns, including safety, user autonomy, privacy, and inclusivity. Through value mapping, stakeholder personas, and ethical pre-mortems, the team surfaces potential value conflicts (e.g., safety vs. autonomy), incorporates diverse knowledge systems (e.g., local trail naming), and ensures transparency and accountability in algorithmic decisions. These discussions result in ethically informed user stories, design constraints, and a shared understanding of responsible innovation practices that guide the subsequent development process.

The PO and the client collaboratively define and prioritizes ethically informed product requirements, which are documented in a shared backlog. This backlog serves as the foundation for sprint planning, where the Scrum Master and development team allocate tasks while acknowledging that long-term ethical concerns such as value trade-offs or transparency features may be monitored across increments regardless of immediate implementation. During daily scrums, ethical discussions are minimal and typically unnecessary, as prior consensus provides a stable framework. At the end of the 4-week sprint, functional increments are reviewed and evaluated with all stakeholders in the sprint review, ensuring that outputs are tested against ethical expectations. We may call this integration of regular "ethics sprints" into agile development, where teams pause to evaluate the ethical implications of features before deployment or continue with "ethical backlog" items. Finally, the sprint retrospective offers a crucial opportunity to assess not only the adequacy of ethical implementation but also whether the deliberative processes fostered a sustainable culture of ethical reflection within the agile team.

While detailing all possible concrete methods to implement ethical deliberation within software development would exceed the scope of this introductory volume, we believe that the conceptual ideas introduced in Chaps. 6 and 7 provide valuable starting points, especially when integrated into foundational processes such as Sprint 0. In particular, the Product Owner (or similar if SCRUM is not used) role emerges as optimally positioned to facilitate and sustain these ethical reflections, bridging stakeholder values with technical execution throughout the development phase. However, we acknowledge that every software-producing organization possesses its unique structures, dynamics, and operational constraints, making universal prescriptions impractical. Each organization will inevitably need to adapt these insights to its specific context. Nevertheless, the methods and principles discussed herein are broadly applicable and adaptable beyond agile frameworks, suitable for diverse development processes. Our use of the avalanche safety app example aimed to concretize these principles; yet, an even more granular perspective that would focus on specific implementation techniques—such as stakeholder workshops, focus groups, and so on—must be tailored by individual practitioners. We trust that readers, equipped with the conceptual tools and guidelines from this book, possess the practical wisdom necessary to implement effective ethical deliberation in their unique organizational environments.

We began this final chapter with a quote from David Hume, so it seems only fitting to conclude our journey with another one:

> *In our reasonings concerning matter of fact, there are all imaginable degrees of assurance, from the highest certainty to the lowest species of moral evidence. A wise man, therefore, proportions his belief to the evidence.*

In our domain of ethical software engineering, we see this as a subtle yet powerful reminder that ethical software development is not algorithmic and certainly not deterministic. It cannot aspire to discover a singular, everlasting solution. Rather, it demands continuous deliberation, a dynamic discourse, and an ongoing process of weighing different possibilities across diverse cases, contexts, and times. Ultimately, the only certainty is this: if organizations place the right people in the right structures, enabling them to recognize and deliberate on ethical issues effectively, they significantly enhance the likelihood of creating software systems that are normatively better—beneficial not only technically but also morally and socially. This book aimed to support those committed to developing software that is not merely functional in an instrumental sense but also ethically informed. If it provided some guidance and shed even a modest light on the complex landscape of ethical software development, we are hopeful and grateful that it has achieved its purpose.

References

Ahlawat, A., Winecoff, A., & Mayer, J. (2024). Minimum viable ethics: From institutionalizing industry AI governance to product impact. *arXiv preprint arXiv:2409.06926*.

Alker, H. R., Jr. (1969). A typology of ecological fallacies. In M. Dogan & S. Rokkan (Eds.), *Quantitative ecological analysis* (pp. 69–86). Massachusetts Institute of Technology.

Athey, S., & Roberts, J. (2001). Organizational design: Decision rights and incentive contracts. *American Economic Review, 91*(2), 200–205.

Blackman, R. (2022). *Ethical machines: Your concise guide to totally unbiased, transparent, and respectful AI*. Harvard Business Press.

Branco, L. (2024, December 27). Sprint Zero: The solid foundation for successful agile projects. *Support to Develop*. Retrieved from https://www.projectmanagement.com/blog-post/77846/sprint-zero%2D%2Dthe-solid-foundation-for-successful-agile-projects-#

Brief, A. P., & Smith-Crowe, K. (2016). Organizations matter. In A. G. Miller (Ed.), *The social psychology of good and evil* (2nd ed., pp. 390–414). The Guilford Press.

Cohen, D. V. (1995). Creating ethical work climates: A socioeconomic perspective. *The Journal of Socio-Economics, 24*(2), 317–343.

De Cremer, D., & Moore, C. (2020). Toward a better understanding of behavioral ethics in the workplace. *Annual Review of Organizational Psychology and Organizational Behavior, 7*, 369–393.

Dijksterhuis, A., & Aarts, H. (2010). Goals, attention, and (un) consciousness. *Annual Review of Psychology, 61*, 467–490.

Dimant, E. (2019). Contagion of pro- and anti-social behavior among peers and the role of social proximity. *Journal of Economic Psychology, 73*, 66–88.

References

Ford, R. C., & Richardson, W. D. (1994). Ethical decision making: A review of the empirical literature. *Journal of Business Ethics, 13*, 205–221.

Francés-Gómez, P., Sacconi, L., & Faillo, M. (2015). Experimental economics as a method for normative business ethics. *Business Ethics: A European Review, 24*, 41–53.

Frémeaux, S., & Voegtlin, C. (2023). Strengthening deliberation in business: Learning from Aristotle's ethics of deliberation. *Business & Society, 62*(4), 824–859.

Gogoll, J., Zuber, N., Kacianka, S., Greger, T., Pretschner, A., & Nida-Rümelin, J. (2021). Ethics in the software development process: From codes of conduct to ethical deliberation. *Philosophy & Technology, 34*, 1085–1108.

Gunia, B. C., Wang, L., Huang, L. I., Wang, J., & Murnighan, J. K. (2012). Contemplation and conversation: Subtle influences on moral decision making. *Academy of Management Journal, 55*(1), 13–33.

Hume, D. (1994). Of the original contract. In K. Haakonssen (Ed.), *Hume: Political essays* (pp. 186–201). Cambridge University Press. (Original work published 1770).

Jackson, R. W., Wood, C. M., & Zboja, J. J. (2013). The dissolution of ethical decision-making in organizations: A comprehensive review and model. *Journal of Business Ethics, 116*(2), 233–250.

Mitnick, B. M. (1995). Systematics and CSR: The theory and processes of normative referencing. *Business & Society, 34*(1), 5–33.

Olsson, T., & Väänänen, K. (2021). How does AI challenge design practice? *Interactions, 28*(4), 62–64.

Partogi, J. (2015, October 1). *Who is the professional Scrum Product Owner*. Scrum.org. Retrieved from https://www.scrum.org/resources/blog/who-professional-scrum-product-owner.

Smith, I. H., & Kouchaki, M. (2021). Ethical learning: The workplace as a moral laboratory for character development. *Social Issues and Policy Review, 15*(1), 277–322.

Tenbrunsel, A. E., Smith-Crowe, K., & Umphress, E. (2003). Building houses on rocks: The role of the ethical infrastructure in organizations. *Social Justice Research, 16*(3), 285–307.

Treviño, L. K., Weaver, G. R., & Reynolds, S. J. (2006). Behavioral ethics in organizations: A review. *Journal of Management, 32*(6), 951–990. https://doi.org/10.1177/0149206306294258

Treviño, L. K., Den Nieuwenboer, N. A., & Kish-Gephart, J. J. (2014). (Un)ethical behavior in organizations. *Annual Review of Psychology, 65*(1), 635–660. https://doi.org/10.1146/annurev-psych-113011-143745

Yu, H., Siegel, J. Z., Clithero, J. A., & Crockett, M. J. (2021). How peer influence shapes value computation in moral decision-making. *Cognition, 211*, 104641.

Zuber, N., Gogoll, J., Kacianka, S., Pretschner, A., & Nida-Rümelin, J. (2022). Empowered and embedded: Ethics and agile processes. *Humanities and Social Sciences Communications, 9*(1), 1–13.

Zuber, N., Gogoll, J., Kacianka, S., Nida-Rümelin, J., & Pretschner, A. (2024). Value-sensitive software design: Ethical deliberation in agile development processes. In H. In Werthner, C. Ghezzi, J. Kramer, J. Nida-Rümelin, B. Nuseibeh, E. Prem, & A. Stanger (Eds.), *Introduction to digital humanism: A textbook* (p. 637). Springer Nature.

Open Access This chapter is licensed under the terms of the Creative Commons Attribution 4.0 International License (http://creativecommons.org/licenses/by/4.0/), which permits use, sharing, adaptation, distribution and reproduction in any medium or format, as long as you give appropriate credit to the original author(s) and the source, provide a link to the Creative Commons license and indicate if changes were made.

The images or other third party material in this chapter are included in the chapter's Creative Commons license, unless indicated otherwise in a credit line to the material. If material is not included in the chapter's Creative Commons license and your intended use is not permitted by statutory regulation or exceeds the permitted use, you will need to obtain permission directly from the copyright holder.

MIX
Papier aus verantwortungsvollen Quellen
Paper from responsible sources
FSC® C105338

If you have any concerns about our products,
you can contact us on
ProductSafety@springernature.com

In case Publisher is established outside the EU,
the EU authorized representative is:
**Springer Nature Customer Service Center GmbH
Europaplatz 3, 69115 Heidelberg, Germany**

Printed by Libri Plureos GmbH
in Hamburg, Germany